_____

By

_____

On the Occasion of

_____

Date

_____

The
EXPERIENCE
of CHRISTMAS

*Family Devotions & Activities
to Prepare the Heart*

LEE WARREN

BARBOUR
PUBLISHING

The
EXPERIENCE
of CHRISTMAS

Published by Barbour Publishing, Inc., P.O. Box 719, Uhrichsville, Ohio 44683 www.barbourbooks.com

Our mission is to publish and distribute inspirational products offering exceptional value and biblical encouragement to the masses.

 Member of the Evangelical Christian Publishers Association

Printed in the United States of America.
5 4 3 2 1

INTRODUCTION

Every year the Christmas season seems to come and go more quickly. In spite of our best intentions and deepest longings, any hope of slowing down to enjoy the real meaning of the season fades with each pressing commitment. We have presents to buy, Christmas parties to attend, food to prepare, and Christmas cards to address.

While we may dream about sitting down with the family in the living room to enjoy beautiful Christmas music while gazing at the tree, in truth, year after year we starve our souls. As Christians, our souls long to drink deeper of the things of Christ—and still we yield to the other demands for our time. In short, we are missing the essence of Christmas.

This year can be different. If your soul longs for more, you *can* experience Christmas.

With this book as your guide, starting on December 1, your family can embark on a month-long journey. . .one that will allow you to experience Christmas in a very meaningful way with the help of traditional and not-so-traditional Christmas scriptures.

Take your time with each devotion. Make it a family event each night as you gather, say, around the dinner table. It's helpful to read through each devotion during your daily quiet time so you can be prepared to help your family gain a deeper appreciation at night.

This book is designed for families with young children *and* those with older ones—with specific sections written for each. Every day you will study one of seven types of devotions: Fulfilled Prophecies, Family Service, Christmas Symbols and Traditions, Christmas Worship, Sharing the Christmas Experience, The Names of the Messiah, and Christmas Prayers.

FULFILLED PROPHECIES

These devotions start with Old Testament prophecies that predict different aspects of the coming Messiah. By exploring how Christ fulfilled those prophecies, your family will develop an appreciation of what God did to orchestrate the miraculous and joyous birth of Christ.

FAMILY SERVICE
Remembering that the Magi brought gifts to offer Jesus with no apparent thought of receiving anything in return, these devotions will help your family to think more about service born out of a love for Christ.

CHRISTMAS SYMBOLS AND TRADITIONS
Christmas symbols and traditions hold rich meaning. These devotions will help you understand and appreciate the scriptural foundation of those symbols and traditions in fresh new ways.

CHRISTMAS WORSHIP
These devotions will help your family acquire the mind-set of wanting to worship Christ. We need to worship Jesus for His willingness to become incarnate so that we might be saved.

SHARING THE CHRISTMAS EXPERIENCE
After the Magi saw the Christ child, they told others what they had seen. Such news was too good to keep to themselves. In that spirit, these devotions encourage families to share the gospel this Christmas season.

THE NAMES OF THE MESSIAH
Isaiah 9 refers to the coming Messiah as "Wonderful Counselor," "Mighty God," "Everlasting Father," and "Prince of Peace." These devotions explore the wonder and majesty of each name and in the process help your family appreciate Jesus more.

CHRISTMAS PRAYERS
These devotions will help your family pursue prayer that is centered around Christmas by following the A(doration), C(onfession), T(hanksgiving), and S(upplication) model.

Each type of devotion, except for Christmas Prayers, contains the following sections:

FAMILY DEVOTION
These one-page devotions are written so that small children can understand them. If your family has older children, reading these devotions is still advisable and probably necessary for your family to enjoy the rest of the material for that day.

GOING DEEPER
These two-page devotions for families with older children dig deeper into the context of the scripture verses. If you have younger children and think they will not benefit from or understand a deeper look at each topic, then feel free to skip these.

FAMILY PRAYER TIME
The prayers in this section are meant to be prayed aloud as a family. The prayers are broken down into prayers for families with young children and families with older children. Pray the prayer that best suits your family. Encourage different family members to lead these prayers or gather around one another and pray them together.

CHRISTMAS CAROL
These Christmas carols correspond with the topic being studied and are intended to be sung together (or read aloud) as a family. If you are unfamiliar with a carol, go to the Cyber Hymnal Web site (www.cyberhymnal.org) and search for that particular carol. When you open the page, the background music will begin to play and you can sing right along. You may want to listen to the tune in advance and then help your family by singing a bar or two until they catch on.

LIVING THE EXPERIENCE
This one-page section contains practical questions for family discussion and family activities that are based upon the topic

you are studying. This is your opportunity as a family to live the Christmas experience. You don't need to discuss every question or participate in every activity. Choose the ones that work best for your family.

The only section that will not follow the model previously described is one called Christmas Prayers. Here's how these types of devotions are broken down:

FAMILY PRAYER
This one-page prayer is written so that young children can understand it. Such prayers are meant to be prayed aloud. Parents of older children may want to skip this section (or pray through both sections).

GOING DEEPER PRAYER
This one-page prayer was written for families with older children. These are meant to be prayed aloud. Parents of younger children may want to skip this section.

MAKING IT PERSONAL
Here you'll find a one-page list of practical suggestions for prayer. Your family will be encouraged to stop and pray right then—sometimes silently and sometimes aloud together.

CLOSING FAMILY PRAYER
This one-page prayer will help your family focus on the things of God during the Christmas season. Have one parent pray this aloud.

When you experience Christmas with Jesus as the focus, every day becomes a gift just waiting to be opened and shared. . . especially with those who have not heard the Good News.

December 1

Fulfilled Prophecies: The Virgin Birth

OLD TESTAMENT PROPHECY:

Therefore the Lord himself will give you a sign.
Behold, the virgin shall conceive and bear a son,
and shall call his name Immanuel.

ISAIAH 7:14

Around seven hundred years before Jesus was born, a man named Isaiah told King Ahaz that a time was coming when a virgin would have a child named Immanuel. Isaiah didn't make this up. He was just telling King Ahaz what God had told him.

Parents who lived during Bible times often chose names for their children that meant something special. Immanuel means "God with us." At that time only men like Isaiah, who was called a *prophet*, could receive messages from God. But amazingly, Isaiah spoke about a time when God would be with people like you and me.

Isaiah's words came true in the first chapter of the Book of Matthew, verses 18 to 23. Matthew writes that an angel appeared to a man named Joseph and told him that the woman he was engaged to, named Mary, was going to have a child named Jesus. This Jesus was actually God's Son, even though He would be born to Mary. The Bible says that Jesus was God in human form. For the first time in history, as Isaiah had said to King Ahaz, God was indeed with us.

GOING DEEPER

King Ahaz was a wicked ruler who even sacrificed his own son in a fire (see 2 Kings 16:1–4). But God intended to preserve what is known as His "remnant," or the family line from Abraham to Jesus (see 2 Kings 19:30–31 and Matthew 1:1–17). Thus, He came to the aid of King Ahaz when Judah was on the verge of war with Syria, which had joined forces with Israel.

Isaiah 7:2 describes the people of Judah as shaking in fear at the prospect of being conquered by Syria and Israel. That's when God sent Isaiah to tell them not to be afraid, calling Syria and Israel "two smoldering stumps of firebrands" (Isaiah 7:4). God, through the prophet Isaiah, proclaimed that He was in complete control and would not allow the attack to take place.

After King Ahaz appeared to show respect for God by saying that he would not test Him (Isaiah 7:12), amazingly, God went even further to save Judah from imminent danger. He told them about the coming Messiah named Immanuel, a name that means "God with us." God was informing His people that He planned to come to earth as a baby so that all of humankind could have access to His saving power.

At this point in Judah's history, God spoke through His prophets, and He accepted animal sacrifices by priests to atone for the sins of His people. But for God to say that He planned to come to earth in the form of a baby and live among His people spoke about a closeness between God and humans that His people had never considered. Needless to say, the people began to get very excited to see the long-awaited Christ child.

Some seven hundred years later, Joseph and Mary, who were from the city of Nazareth, were engaged to be married. Mary, still a virgin, was "found to be with child from the Holy Spirit" (Matthew 1:18). An angel of the Lord appeared to Joseph in a dream and told him that his wife-to-be would deliver the Christ child.

The wait was over. The Messiah was about to be born

and God would no longer dwell in tents or tabernacles. Instead, He would live and eat and walk among both kings and commoners.

As you begin to look forward to Christmas, rejoice that your Savior, King, and God loved you enough to take on flesh and be born as a baby in a world full of sinners.

FAMILY PRAYER TIME

For Families with Young Children:
Father, our family is already looking forward to celebrating the birth of the baby Jesus. Thank You for keeping the promise You made to King Ahaz to send us Your Son. Thank You for loving us enough to come to earth to live among us. Amen.

For Families with Older Children:
Father, as we begin the season in which we meditate upon the glorious and wondrous birth of Your Son, we believe that You still dwell among your people. Draw us closer as a family by visiting us with Your presence this very day, O Immanuel. Amen.

O Come, O Come, Emmanuel

(Selected verses)
Author unknown

O come, O come, Emmanuel,
And ransom captive Israel,
That mourns in lonely exile here
Until the Son of God appear.

Refrain:
Rejoice! Rejoice!
Emmanuel shall come to thee, O Israel.

O come, Thou Wisdom from on high,
Who orderest all things mightily;
To us the path of knowledge show,
And teach us in her ways to go. (Refrain)

O come, Thou Rod of Jesse, free
Thine own from Satan's tyranny;
From depths of hell Thy people save,
And give them victory over the grave. (Refrain)

O come, Thou Day-spring, come and cheer
Our spirits by Thine advent here;
Disperse the gloomy clouds of night,
And death's dark shadows put to flight. (Refrain)

O come, Thou Key of David, come,
And open wide our heavenly home;
Make safe the way that leads on high,
And close the path to misery. (Refrain)

Family Discussion Topics:

❧ Why is God faithful to His remnant even when they aren't faithful to Him?

❧ What would it have been like to be alive during the seven hundred years between Isaiah's prophecy about the coming Messiah and Jesus' birth? Would you have given up hope, or would you have clung to God's promise?

❧ Why is it important that God is "with us"?

Family Activities:

❧ Write an additional verse for "O Come, O Come, Emmanuel."

❧ Use a nativity scene to reenact the birth of Christ. Start with an empty stable except for the animals for now. Move the wise men and the shepherds somewhere else (to symbolize their distance from Jesus). Put Joseph and Mary far away from the stable—maybe even in another room (to symbolize their home in Nazareth far from Bethlehem). Hide the angels and the baby Jesus until Christmas morning.

DECEMBER 2

FAMILY SERVICE:
THE BRECI FAMILY

And the King will answer them, "Truly, I say to you, as you did it to one of the least of these my brothers, you did it to me."
MATTHEW 25:40

FAMILY DEVOTION

Logan and Kayleigh are just like other children at Christmas. They can't wait to open their gifts and see what neat things are inside. Like most boys, Logan wants things like skateboards, iPods, and video games. Kayleigh wants makeup, computer software, and cool clothes.

A few years ago their parents, Randy and Deana, began to wonder if maybe Logan and Kayleigh were starting to forget that Christmas is about Jesus. After all, Christmas is more than a day to get presents.

One day Randy stopped at a place called the Child Saving Institute (or CSI) that he'd driven by many times. He found out that they take care of children who are up for adoption, have been abandoned, or are in a bad home situation. He also found out that they collect and give toys to these children at Christmastime.

Logan and Kayleigh's family started a new tradition that year. Logan and Kayleigh decided to give up at least one new toy to take to the CSI. Doing something for somebody in need is like doing it for Jesus.

GOING DEEPER

In Matthew 25, Jesus paints a picture of what Judgment Day will look like. He said that He will divide what He calls the "sheep" from the "goats." Sheep are Jesus' followers. Goats are unbelievers. After Jesus has separated them, He will call His sheep into His kingdom that was prepared for them from the foundation of the world.

Jesus knows His followers. By helping other people, Jesus said they are helping Him. Here are Jesus' exact words from Matthew 25:35–36: "For I was hungry and you gave me food, I was thirsty and you gave me drink, I was a stranger and you welcomed me, I was naked and you clothed me, I was sick and you visited me, I was in prison and you came to me."

Jesus identifies with people who are hurting, abandoned, and abused. He experienced all three situations on the cross, and He continues to experience them every time one person is in need.

Your family can help meet the needs of people in many different ways throughout the year. What better way to serve Jesus right now than to help children at Christmastime?

Most communities have organizations like the Child Saving Institute that Randy and Deana Breci and their children help each year. This one particular institute helped 2,480 children and their families in some fashion in 2004. That's just one institute in one city.

The need is great, and most of us have an abundance of things—more than we'll ever need or use. If every Christian family did what the Brecis are doing each Christmas, organizations like CSI would be able to provide an abundance of toys for every child in their care.

If you aren't sure where to start, ask your pastor. Maybe your family could even start a toy drive in your own church. That way you'd be giving other people in your church the opportunity to minister to hurting children in Jesus' name.

For Families with Young Children:

Father, help us to remember the children in our city who will not receive any gifts this Christmas. Help us to care more about those children than we do about receiving gifts. We know that when we give to meet the needs of others, we are really helping Jesus. Amen.

For Families with Older Children:

Father, we often spend more time thinking about what we're going to receive at Christmas than what we're going to do for others. We ask for the same compassion that Jesus has for those who are downtrodden or in pain. Father, shape us into a family of sheep who ministers to the basic needs of others. We know that when we do so, we are doing it unto You. Amen.

Father, Our Hearts We Lift

(Selected verses)
Words by Charles Wesley

Father, our hearts we lift,
Up to Thy gracious throne,
And bless Thee for the precious gift,
Of Thine incarnate Son;
The gift unspeakable,
We thankfully receive,
And to the world Thy goodness tell,
And to Thy glory live.

Jesus the holy Child,
Doth by His birth declare,
That God and men are reconciled,
And one in Him we are;
Salvation through His Name
To all mankind is giv'n,
And loud His infant cries proclaim
A peace 'twixt earth and heav'n.

His kingdom from above,
He doth to us impart,
And pure benevolence and love,
O'erflow the faithful heart;
Changèd in a moment we
The sweet attraction find,
With open arms of charity
Embracing all mankind.

Family Discussion Topics:

❧ Does your family spend too much time thinking about the gifts you're going to receive at Christmas? If so, how did this attitude develop in your family?

❧ If works have nothing to do with our salvation, as Paul said in Ephesians 2:8–9, then why does Jesus make such a big deal about works when He talks about separating the sheep from the goats?

Family Activities:

❧ Call a few local charities to find out if they hold toy drives for disadvantaged children. Pray about which one your family should help, and then follow through.

❧ Talk to your pastor about starting a toy drive at your church.

❧ Get involved with Prison Fellowship's Angel Tree program that collects and distributes gifts to children who have parents in prison (or talk to your pastor about getting your church involved in this ministry). For more information, go to http://www.angeltree.org.

DECEMBER 3

CHRISTMAS SYMBOLS AND TRADITIONS: CHRISTMAS WREATHS

*The Lord is merciful and gracious, slow to anger
and abounding in steadfast love.*
PSALM 103:8

Family Devotion

Have you seen Christmas wreaths hanging on front doors in your neighborhood during Christmas? Maybe you have one on your own house. Some Christian families place a wreath with candles on their kitchen or dining room table during Christmas. They light one new candle every week as they await Jesus' birthday.

The Christmas wreath, which is round like a circle, is supposed to remind us that God's kindness has no beginning or end. Isn't that a beautiful picture?

When someone hurts you, you probably get upset, and you don't want to be friends with that person anymore. Even so, God says that you should "forgive" that person. Unlike us, God is slow to get angry, and He is always forgiving.

God has known from the beginning of the world that people would often choose to do the wrong things. That's why He sent His only Son, Jesus, to earth. God knew that Jesus would be killed for the sins, or bad thoughts and actions, of the world. When Jesus died and rose again three days later, God's kindness—what we call mercy—became available to everyone.

Going Deeper

In 1833 a Christian man named Johann Hinrich Wichern opened an orphanage called The Rough House near Hamburg, Germany. One year as the Christmas season approached, Wichern wanted to find a way to help the children in the orphanage understand Christmas in a fresh and meaningful way.

He came up with the idea of a wooden ring or chandelier that would contain candles. During prayer time each night, the children would light one candle in anticipation of the coming of the baby Jesus. The light from the candles represented Jesus, whom the scriptures call the "light of the world," and the ring came to symbolize God's eternal mercy that has no beginning or end.

Originally, the ring, which was decorated with evergreens, is believed to have started out with twenty-four small red candles and four larger white candles (lighted on Sundays). Over the next hundred years, similar wreaths began showing up in homes across Germany. Eventually, people began to believe that the evergreen portion of the wreath symbolized God's faithfulness to His people by granting them eternal life.

While wreaths existed before 1833 and were used by pre-Christian cultures in Europe to commemorate the winter solstice, Wichern and many believers after him embraced and changed the use of wreaths to give the Christmas season more meaning for believers.

Today people create "advent wreaths" in their homes to look forward to the coming Messiah, much as the children of The Rough House did nearly two hundred years ago. The wreaths of today often have fewer candles (four or five) and are lighted on each Sunday in December. Some Christian denominations have changed the color of the candles to three violet (or blue) candles that represent sorrow and longing, and one red (or pink) candle that represents hope. Occasionally, you may see an extra candle in the middle of the wreath that is white and a little larger than the other candles. It is lighted on Christmas Day.

However a family or church decides to use Christmas wreaths, whether on the kitchen table or hanging from a front door, the beauty of the symbolism is powerful. While we were still sinners, God sent His only Son to earth to die so that we might have eternal life. Like the Christmas wreath, God's mercy is everlasting.

FAMILY PRAYER TIME

For Families with Young Children:

Father, thank You for being slow to anger and for being patient with us when we do bad things. We look forward to Christmas this year because we know that if Jesus hadn't come to earth as a baby, He wouldn't have died for our sins and we wouldn't be able to enter heaven. Amen.

For Families with Older Children:

Father, You are a merciful, patient God who doesn't give us what we deserve—everlasting punishment. Instead, through the death of Your Son on the cross, You offer us eternal life. We consciously and reverently look forward to Christmas this year, which is the celebration of the day that You chose to reveal Yourself to us. Help us to continually remember Your patience and mercy as we grow in the faith. Amen.

O Mercy Divine, O Couldst Thou Incline

(Selected verses)

Words by Charles Wesley

O mercy divine, O couldst Thou incline,
My God, to become such as infant as mine?
What wonder of grace: The Ancient of Days
Is found in the likeness of Adam's frail race!

He comes from on high, who fashioned the sky,
And meekly vouchsafes in a manger to lie;
Our God ever blest, with oxen doth rest,
Is nursed by His creature and hangs at the breast.

So heavenly-mild, His innocence smiled,
No wonder the mother would worship the Child,
The angels she knew had worshipped Him, too,
And still they confess adoration His due.

On Jesus' face, with eager amaze,
And pleasure ecstatic the cherubim gaze;
Their newly born King, transported they sing,
And Heaven and earth with the triumph doth ring.

The shepherds behold Him, the promised of old,
By angels attended, by prophets foretold;
The wise men adore now, and bring Him their store,
The rich are permitted to follow the poor.

To the inn they repair, to see the young Heir;
The inn is a palace, for Jesus is there!
Who now would be great, and not rather wait
On Jesus their Lord in His humble estate?

Family Discussion Topics:

❧ In what ways has God been merciful and slow to anger with your family?

❧ How might a Christmas wreath help your family better appreciate the season?

Family Activities:

❧ Purchase a Christmas wreath with candles and spend time around it each night as a family—taking turns lighting the candles. Make this the highlight of your day as you pray together as a family and look forward to celebrating the birth of Christ.

❧ Tell another family about the meaning of Christmas wreaths.

❧ Commit the different symbols of the wreath to memory.

DECEMBER 4

CHRISTMAS WORSHIP:
WISE MEN WORSHIP

*And going into the house they [the wise men]
saw the child with Mary his mother, and they
fell down and worshiped him. Then, opening their
treasures, they offered him gifts, gold and
frankincense and myrrh.*

MATTHEW 2:11

FAMILY DEVOTION

When wise men who came from a land east of Jerusalem realized that Jesus had been born, they traveled to see Him for themselves. They wanted to worship Him and bring Him gifts. To the wise men, Jesus was a king.

We don't know a lot about these wise men, but we do know that when they met with King Herod, he became upset. If the wise men wanted to worship another king, Herod thought his people might do the same.

So King Herod gathered many of God's people to hear what they had to say regarding the coming of the long promised Messiah. They told him that indeed Jesus was the Messiah that Old Testament saints predicted would come some day.

As much as Herod didn't like the arrival of Jesus, he could do nothing to stop the wise men from worshiping Jesus. When they saw Jesus, the Bible says they fell down (maybe to their knees or maybe all the way to the ground) and worshiped the Christ child. And in so doing, they celebrated the first Christmas.

GOING DEEPER

The wise men who saw a star and came to worship Jesus are still a mystery to us. We know that they weren't part of God's people, Israel. We know that they were scholars. And we know that they were often referred to as *Magou* or *Magi*, which means "magician." Some believe that they came from Arabia since scripture refers to that land as "the east" (Genesis 25:6; Judges 6:3).

No matter who the Magi were, we know that God

drew them to His Son with a star that captured their attention. In Matthew 2:2, the Magi referred to the star as "his star," in reference to Christ being called the "king of the Jews." So, in God's sovereignty, they knew they were being drawn to Christ.

King Herod had no intention of being dethroned, so after conferring with the chief priests and scribes to confirm that these events were truly those predicted by the Old Testament saints about the coming Messiah, he tried to fool the Magi into leading him to where Jesus lay. Herod wanted to kill the baby Jesus.

After the Magi spoke to the king, God allowed them to see the star once again and it led them straight to "the place where the child was" (Matthew 2:9). The next verse says that "they rejoiced exceedingly with great joy" when they saw the star. They knew that the baby Jesus was close, and they couldn't contain themselves. Their joy bubbled over.

Imagine how they felt as they approached the building where Mary lay cradling Jesus in her arms. "They fell down and worshiped him." What a reason to celebrate!

Their worship led to a heart of giving. They offered Christ gifts of gold, frankincense, and myrrh. Some believe that the gold symbolized a rendering of payment as befitting of a king, the frankincense symbolized the sweet fragrance of the sacrificial death of Christ, and the myrrh, a spice used to treat dead bodies, symbolized a man who was destined to die. Others, like Bible commentator Matthew Henry, see the gifts as more of a sign of God's providence sent to bring financial relief to

Joseph and Mary who were poor at the time.

Whatever the reason, the Magi's spirit of worship led to giving Christ, and not each other, gifts. Maybe all of us should be a little more focused on what we can offer Christ and less concerned with what we'll receive on His birthday.

FAMILY PRAYER TIME

For Families with Young Children:

Father, we come to You today just as the wise men came so many years ago. We come because we want to worship Your Son and because we want to offer our service as a family to Him. This Christmas, help us understand that Jesus is the reason for Christmas and not the presents we hope to receive. Amen.

For Families with Older Children:

Father, just as You pointed the wise men to Christ, we thank You for showing us the way to salvation. May we never take Your gift for granted, and may we always respond to Jesus the way the wise men did when they fell down in worship to Your Son. We remember their gifts, which befitted a king, a Messiah, and a sacrificial lamb that was headed to the slaughter. Amen.

The First Noel
(Selected verses)
Author unknown

The first Noel the angel did say
Was to certain poor shepherds in fields as they lay;
In fields where they lay tending their sheep,
On a cold winter's night that was so deep.

Refrain:
Noel, Noel, Noel, Noel,
Born is the King of Israel.

They lookèd up and saw a star
Shining in the east, beyond them far;
And to the earth it gave great light,
And so it continued both day and night. (Refrain)

And by the light of that same star
Three Wise Men came from country far;
To seek for a King was their intent,
And to follow the star wherever it went. (Refrain)

This star drew nigh to the northwest,
Over Bethlehem it took its rest;
And there it did both stop and stay,
Right over the place where Jesus lay. (Refrain)

Then entered in those Wise Men three,
Full reverently upon the knee,
And offered there, in His presence,
Their gold and myrrh and frankincense. (Refrain)

Family Discussion Topics:

❧ How much does your family resemble the wise men in their attitudes to seek and then worship Jesus during Christmas?

❧ Is your family usually more focused on giving to Jesus or to each other during Christmas?

❧ What might your family do for, or give, Jesus this Christmas season?

Family Activities:

❧ Just as the Magi fell down to worship Christ, spend time as a family on your knees in a brief time of prayer or in singing your favorite family hymn.

❧ Make an agreement among your family to spend less on each other's gifts this year (or to purchase one less gift for each other). Send the difference to a worthy cause.

December 5

Sharing the Christmas Experience: Shepherds Evangelize

*And when they saw it, they [the shepherds]
made known the saying that had been told them
concerning this child. And all who heard it
wondered at what the shepherds told them.*
Luke 2:17-18

FAMILY DEVOTION

Can you remember the last time you heard good news? Maybe you received an A on a homework assignment, or you were made a leader in your class during vacation Bible school. You could hardly wait to tell everybody.

When something good happens to you, *not* telling someone is almost impossible. That's how the shepherds felt. After they saw the baby Jesus, they had to go tell others the good news.

Sometimes when we tell others our good news, they don't seem very excited. But that didn't happen to the shepherds. In fact, all the people who heard their good news about Jesus "wondered" (or as some Bibles say, "marveled") at what they heard.

Do you have friends who celebrate Christmas but don't understand why? If so, tell them that Christmas is about the birth of Jesus and that He came to save them from their bad thoughts and actions. God may cause them to "marvel" at your words.

GOING DEEPER

As shepherds tended fields in the Bethlehem region on the day that Jesus was born, God sent them an angel to proclaim this news: "For unto you is born this day in the city of David a Savior, who is Christ the Lord" (Luke 2:11).

Shepherds were not looked upon favorably for many reasons. Often poor, they were unable to satisfy the chief priests because their work made them ceremonially unclean. They were also considered to be plain, ordinary people without any social or political status.

For those reasons, the shepherds likely were stunned when God chose to reveal Himself to them through an angel. They probably would have expected the chief priests to be the first to hear about the birth of the Messiah. But God is in the business of lifting up the humble and crushing the proud.

We don't know whether the shepherds met the Magi as they traveled to see Jesus. All we are sure of is that God chose two very distinct and different groups (the Magi and the shepherds) to reveal the most glorious event in the history of humankind—the day that God became man and dwelt among us.

After seeing the Christ child for themselves, the shepherds had to share their discovery (Luke 2:17–18). They began telling many others in the region about what they heard from the angels and what they saw in the manger. And all those who heard their stories marveled at the news.

Most people, even those who are not yet believers, seem much more open to hearing about Christ during the Christmas season. They've sung the Christmas carols about the birth of Christ. They're accustomed to seeing nativity scenes. And they know that the season is intended to be about the birth of Jesus.

But just because a person is more open to the spirit of the season doesn't make him or her a Christian. Each year at this time, we have a marvelous opportunity to do what the shepherds did—to tell others that the Savior of the world has been born and that He is worthy to be honored and adored.

For Families with Young Children:

Father, we know people at school and in our neighborhood who celebrate Christmas but they don't really know why. When we see how excited the shepherds were to share that the Messiah had been born, we want to do the same. Give us opportunities this Christmas to be as bold as the shepherds in sharing our faith. Amen.

For Families with Older Children:

Father, when we read about the shepherds' encounter with an angel in Luke 2, we rejoice in knowing that You are a God who makes Himself available to all kinds of people. Just as the shepherds were unable to keep the good news about the birth of the Messiah to themselves, we, too, long to make Your saving power known in our community. And we long to see people marvel over You. Help us to share the Christmas experience with others this season. Amen.

Go, Tell It on the Mountain

Words by John W. Work Jr.

Refrain:
Go, tell it on the mountain,
Over the hills and everywhere
Go, tell it on the mountain,
That Jesus Christ is born.

While shepherds kept their watching
Over silent flocks by night
Behold throughout the heavens
There shone a holy light. (Refrain)

The shepherds feared and trembled,
When lo! above the earth,
Rang out the angels chorus
That hailed the Savior's birth. (Refrain)

Down in a lowly manger
The humble Christ was born
And God sent us salvation
That blessèd Christmas morn. (Refrain)

Family Discussion Topics:

- ❧ Are you as quick to share the gospel with people as you are in sharing your other good news? Why?

- ❧ Why do most unbelievers celebrate Christmas? How quick are you to lovingly tell others why you celebrate Christmas?

- ❧ What part does fear play in your unwillingness to tell others about the real meaning of Christmas? How might this scripture passage help you to work through your fear?

Family Activities:

- ❧ Make a list of neighbors' names and commit to praying for a chance to share the gospel with each of them.

- ❧ Join a group of Christmas carolers who go door-to-door singing about the real meaning of Christmas. If you can't find a group, then start one of your own.

DECEMBER 6

THE NAMES OF THE MESSIAH:
WONDERFUL COUNSELOR

For to us a child is born, to us a son is given; and the government shall be upon his shoulder, and his name shall be called Wonderful Counselor, Mighty God, Everlasting Father, Prince of Peace.
ISAIAH 9:6

FAMILY DEVOTION

The prophet Isaiah said that Jesus would be called "Wonderful Counselor"—and today we know Jesus to be both wonderful and a counselor.

Jesus' birth was wonderful, being born of the Virgin Mary. His earthly ministry was wonderful, because He willingly died so we could live with God in heaven forever. And when he went back up into heaven, that was wonderful, too, because He overcame death to do so.

Jesus has always been a counselor, or someone who points to the ways of God as being right and true. After He went back up into heaven, Jesus even sent another counselor to be with us. That counselor is the Holy Spirit who lives within us, guiding us and helping us make the right decisions.

When you think about the baby Jesus this Christmas, spend some time thanking Him for being your Wonderful Counselor.

GOING DEEPER

Some translations of the Bible separate the words *Wonderful* and *Counselor* with a comma and some translations put the two words together. Because the original Hebrew language doesn't use the same punctuation that we use in English, it's difficult to know whether the two terms belong together. However, many theologians group the words together without punctuation because the other titles for Jesus in this passage contain two words.

We know Jesus to be wonderful. His name is above every other name—so much so that demons tremble at the very mention of it. And we know His counsel to be perfect because He has always existed with the Father and the Holy Spirit and He speaks only those words that come from the Father.

When we combine the titles of *Wonderful* and *Counselor*, we have a Savior who speaks and acts with such authority that we should cower in fear at His every command. As this passage says, God has even put the government upon the shoulders of the Messiah, and of the increase of His government and peace, there shall be no end.

And then we read this: "Unto *us*" a child is born. The Messiah's absolute authority is clothed in His love for us, so much so that He came to us as a baby.

At Christmas you may find it difficult to think of Jesus as one who had authority from on high because as an infant He appeared to be so vulnerable. But in reality, the Father protected Him at every turn, first from King Herod and then from the Sanhedrin, who desired to kill Jesus early in His earthly ministry. Even when Jesus was crucified, He didn't die at the hands of Roman soldiers or the Sanhedrin, but rather of His own will—and only precisely at God's appointed time.

When you meditate about the miraculous birth of Jesus this Christmas, understand that you are not merely worshiping a Messiah who came to earth by way of a miraculous birth. Instead, you are worshiping the Wonderful Counselor whose miraculous ministry carries with it the authority and majesty that is due to such a name.

For Families with Young Children:

Father, we thank You for the Wonderful Counselor. We know Jesus to be both wonderful in His love for us and a perfect counselor—in whom only the truth lies. As our family celebrates the birth of Jesus this Christmas, help us to remember that He willingly left heaven, took on human skin, and lived among us. He gave us a perfect example of the Christian life, and then He died on the cross so that we could spend eternity with Him. Amen.

For Families with Older Children:

Father, when we think about eternity, it's difficult for us to grasp. To know that our Savior has always been with You and that He willingly left Your perfect dwelling place to save us from our sins is overwhelming. We acknowledge and rejoice that the name of Jesus is above every other name—in heaven and on earth. We worship the Christ child this Christmas knowing that He is, was, and always will be the Wonderful Counselor. Amen.

For Unto Us a Child Is Born

Words by Susan H. Peterson

For unto us a child is born,
To us a son is giv'n;
The government shall rest on him,
Th' anointed One from heav'n.
His name is Wonderful Counselor,
The Mighty God is He,
The Everlasting Father,
The humble Prince of Peace.

The increase of his government
And peace shall never end;
He'll reign on David's ancient throne
As ruler of all men.
Upheld with justice and righteousness,
Forever his kingdom will last;
The zeal of the Lord God Most High
Will bring these things to pass.

Lord Jesus, come now and reign in me,
Be Lord of my life this hour.
Come be my Counselor and my God,
My source of wisdom and power.
Watch o'er me with your Father care,
My heart and my mind, fill with peace.
I worship you, my Lord and King,
My praise will never cease.

Family Discussion Topics:

❧ In what ways is Jesus a Wonderful Counselor?

❧ How does having Jesus as your Wonderful Counselor change or enrich your life?

❧ What did Isaiah mean when he said that the government would be upon Jesus' shoulders?

Family Activities:

❧ Play a recording of Handel's *Messiah* or attend a live performance. Some performances encourage families to sing along with the choir.

❧ Read the following passages: John 14:16, John 14:26, John 15:26, and John 16:7. Then take a couple of minutes to thank God for sending the promised Counselor.

December 7

Christmas Prayers:
Adoration

It will be said on that day, "Behold, this is our God; we have waited for him, that he might save us. This is the LORD; we have waited for him; let us be glad and rejoice in his salvation."

Isaiah 25:9

FAMILY PRAYER

Father, we adore You this Christmas for sending Your only Son to earth so that we could live with You forever. We can't imagine how hard that must have been. We know that You sent Jesus because You love us.

You knew that we would never follow You as we should. Knowing that we do not deserve Your love makes us appreciate what You did for us even more.

We love You and offer You our praise this Christmas. We praise You for loving us when we are so undeserving. We praise You for not leaving us to die in our sin but for having compassion on us. We praise You for coming in the form of a baby so that You could show us how to live as Christians.

We love You for Your mercy, grace, fairness, and peace—all of which can be found in the baby Jesus. And we adore You for sending Jesus to make a way to heaven when one did not exist. Amen.

GOING DEEPER PRAYER

Father, we know that before the foundation of the world You existed three-in-one and that You had a plan to redeem us from our sin from the beginning. We also know that Your dwelling place is perfect and free from sin. For You to leave such perfection so that we might be saved overwhelms us with joy.

We join with the Magi and the shepherds in wanting to worship God who came in the form of a baby. We know that our offerings of sacrifice and praise grant us no security. Instead, we offer You our praise simply because we are awed by Your love for us. In You we find all the security we'll ever need.

As we draw closer to Christmas, give our family a greater sense of admiration, wonder, and awe for the Christ child. Give us the desire to praise and worship You in all that we do, say, and think. For we know that even the ability to give You praise comes from You and not ourselves.

May our adoration for You be so clear to the unbelieving world that they wonder about the source of such joy. And may we be prepared to tell them that only in You do we live, move, and have our being. Amen.

MAKING IT PERSONAL

Have a time of silent prayer about one or more of the following:

- ❧ Ask God to increase your desire to praise Christ and the work He has done in your life—and to decrease your desire to take credit for what He has done.

- ❧ Ask God if you have any sin that you've been holding onto that may be keeping you from worshiping the Christ child as you know you should.

- ❧ Praise and adore Christ for anything He has done for you this week that you haven't already acknowledged.

- ❧ Spend a minute meditating on what the first Christmas Day was like.

- ❧ Praise God for His willingness to accept your praises

and adoration this Christmas season—knowing that you are not deserving of such acceptance apart from Christ.

CLOSING FAMILY PRAYER

Father, this Christmas we are looking forward to the customs of the season—to family traditions, parties, gift exchanges, and great meals. While nothing is inherently wrong with any of those things, we desire a deeper, richer, and fuller experience with the Lover of our souls.

When our family begins to stray from a sense of wonder and adoration this Christmas, be quick to show us. When we begin to get caught up in all of the festivities of the season, remind us that the birth of Your Son is the sole reason we are celebrating. When we desire to spend more time involved in activities than we do in reverent adoration of Your Son, remind us that we were created for worship.

We want more of Jesus and less of the things of this world. We want to experience His presence, to walk in His ways, and to know Him more intimately than we do any human.

Give us a spirit of adoration for the Savior this Christmas that transforms our every activity into one of worship. Give us a spirit of praise that sets us free from anything that entangles us. And above all, Father, help us never to lose the wonder of Christmas Day. Without Christmas we would be lost in our sin and without hope. Amen.

DECEMBER 8

FULFILLED PROPHECIES:
THE DIVINITY OF CHRIST

OLD TESTAMENT PROPHECY:

But you, O Bethlehem Ephrathah, who are too little to be among the clans of Judah, from you shall come forth for me one who is to be ruler in Israel, whose origin is from of old, from ancient days.
MICAH 5:2

In human terms, what Micah said didn't make much sense. First, Bethlehem was a small town and not an important place. How could a ruler of Israel come from there? Then Micah said that the ruler would be someone who was "from of old." What does that mean?

At the time, Micah was writing about an event that wouldn't take place for many hundreds of years. One day, though, his words would come true. When Jesus was born, King Herod and his chief priests and scribes recognized that Jesus' birth had been predicted by Micah (see Matthew 2:6).

Just as Micah had written, Jesus—who has always existed in heaven with His Father and the Holy Spirit— came to earth in the form of a baby and was born to Joseph and Mary in the town of Bethlehem.

Thirty years later Jesus began His earthly ministry in Israel—again just as Micah predicted. He established His church and is still ruling God's people today.

GOING DEEPER

At the time of Micah's prediction about the coming Messiah, God was on the verge of sending His people into Babylonia, where they would spend the next seventy years in captivity. Micah 3:9–12 chronicles the reasons for God's judgment against His people—they detested justice, made crooked all that is straight, shed blood, and accepted bribes.

God promised to make Jerusalem into "a heap of ruins" (Micah 3:12), but He also gave Israel reason for hope. God said that a time was coming when "the house of the LORD shall be established as the highest of the mountains, and it shall be lifted up above the hills; and peoples shall flow to it, and many nations shall come. . ." (Micah 4:1–2).

When God restored His people, God said He would become the God of many nations. In fact, Micah 4:2 goes on as follows: "Many nations shall come, and say: 'Come, let us go up to the mountain of the LORD, to the house of the God of Jacob, that he may teach us his ways and that we may walk in his paths.' "

Micah then gets specific about how God would accomplish His plans. He would bring a ruler "whose origin is from of old, from ancient days" out of Bethlehem—a city that was so small that it doesn't even appear in Joshua's list of Judean cities after Israel conquered Canaan (Joshua 15:21).

Only one man in the history of humankind could fit that description. Jesus has always existed with the Father and the Holy Spirit. All three were present and active at the creation of the world (see Genesis 1:26 and Colossians 1:16). That same Jesus, from the ancient days, left heaven to be born in Bethlehem to a young couple named Joseph and Mary.

Jesus established His church and promised that the gates of hell would not prevail against it (Matthew 16:18). His church has been growing ever since. And we're already seeing a partial fulfillment of Micah's prediction that many nations would come to Christ and "walk in his paths" (Micah 4:2).

As you celebrate the birth of Christ this year, rejoice in His patience as He gathers the nations to Himself. Rejoice in His authority to rule and reign for all eternity. And rejoice that the one from of old redeemed your soul.

FAMILY PRAYER TIME

For Families with Young Children:

Father, we see Your faithfulness to keep the promises You made to Your people to give them a Savior. Thank You for being faithful even when Your people are not. Thank You for loving us so much that You sent Your only Son to a lowly place like Bethlehem to be born, and eventually to die for our sins. Amen.

For Families with Older Children:

Father, we see the intricate plan You put in place to redeem us. We are overwhelmed by Your love. We know that Israel deserved judgment—much like we do—and that, in Your righteousness, You delivered them over to Babylonia. In Your mercy, though, You told them that one day You would deliver them with a Savior "from of old." We worship the Christ child today, knowing Him to be the perfect fulfillment of Your servant Micah's prophecy. Amen.

O Little Town of Bethlehem
Words by Phillips Brooks

O little town of Bethlehem, how still we see thee lie!
Above thy deep and dreamless sleep the silent stars go by.
Yet in thy dark streets shineth the everlasting Light;
The hopes and fears of all the years are met in thee tonight.

For Christ is born of Mary, and gathered all above, while
Mortals sleep, the angels keep their watch of wondering love.
O morning stars together, proclaim the holy birth,
And praises sing to God the King, and peace to men on earth!

How silently, how silently, the wondrous Gift is giv'n;
So God imparts to human hearts the blessings of His Heav'n.
No ear may hear His coming, but in this world of sin,
Where meek souls will receive Him still, the dear Christ enters in.

Where children pure and happy pray to the blessèd Child,
Where misery cries out to Thee, Son of the mother mild;
Where charity stands watching and faith holds wide the door,
The dark night wakes, the glory breaks, and Christmas comes
once more.

O holy Child of Bethlehem, descend to us, we pray;
Cast out our sin, and enter in, be born in us today.
We hear the Christmas angels the great glad tidings tell;
O come to us, abide with us, our Lord Emmanuel!

Family Discussion Topics:

❧ Could any other person except Jesus be the promised Messiah, given that God said that the Messiah would be "from ancient days"?

❧ Why did God choose such a small and seemingly insignificant town like Bethlehem for the site of Jesus' birth?

❧ How might God's promise to establish a Messiah have brought comfort to God's people as they entered the Babylonian captivity?

Family Activities:

❧ If you have a family tree, look at it in the context of God's faithfulness from one generation to the next. Make the connection between your family and what God did to orchestrate the birth of Christ.

❧ If you're using a nativity scene to reenact the birth of Christ (see the December 1 devotion), move the wise men and the shepherds closer than you had them before. And then move Joseph and Mary closer as well. Continue to hide the angels and the baby Jesus until Christmas morning.

DECEMBER 9

FAMILY SERVICE:
THE MILLS FAMILY

"You shall love the Lord your God with all your heart and with all your soul and with all your strength and with all your mind, and your neighbor as yourself."
LUKE 10:27

FAMILY DEVOTION

Nearly forty years ago, Charley Mills, his wife Ann, and their two children who were five and three at the time, began a family tradition during Christmas. They wanted to show people in their community how much they loved them.

The week before Christmas, the Mills family bought a small Christmas tree. Then they began baking gingerbread men and sugar cookies and inserted hooks into each one. When they had decorated the tree with the goodies, they put the tree in the car, along with some of the children's nicer toys. They then drove to a children's ward in a nearby hospital.

"We would decorate the tree with the goodies with the help of some of the hospitalized children who were able to do so, give out the toys, and sing carols while we worked," Ann said.

"I would tell or read the story of Jesus' birth, and we would leave extra tins of cookies and refills of the garlands and candy canes for the nurses to replenish the tree when needed.

"We were told that the tree would sometimes be moved into the waiting room, just outside, where it brought joy to some of the families of the hospitalized children, as well."

GOING DEEPER

In Luke 10 a lawyer asked Jesus what he had to do to inherit eternal life. Jesus asked the man about his take on the law of God. The man responded with our theme verse for the day, Luke 10:27: "You shall love the Lord your God with all your heart and with all your soul and with all your strength and with all your mind, and your neighbor as yourself."

After Jesus told the lawyer that he was right, the man wanted to know who his neighbor was. Jesus told him the story about the Samaritan who helped a man who had been beaten, robbed, and left for dead on the side of the road. The Samaritan did not know the man in need, but Jesus considered them to be neighbors. He then told the lawyer to imitate the Samaritan's mercy (verse 37).

The Mills family didn't know the patients in the children's hospital ward in their community. But they knew that these children were their neighbors and that they could do something to help their neighbors enjoy Christmas a little more.

In the process of meeting the needs of people, Charley and Ann wanted to teach their children that meeting needs ought always to be done with the golden rule in mind.

"We taught them that they must 'make room' for the gifts 'Santa' might bring by sharing their present toys with children less fortunate than they," Ann said. "We also encouraged them to select not the old, bedraggled stuffed animals, dolls, and toys to give away but to 'do unto others. . .' by giving only ones that they might be pleased to receive if the tables were turned."

They continued this family tradition all the way into their children's young adult years. Ann said that her family considered it an important part of their family Christmas each year. By being so willing to love their neighbors when it would have been much easier to simply love themselves and their own festivities, they found deeper meaning and enjoyment in Christmas. And in the process, they touched the lives of many people in the name of the Savior, who wouldn't have experienced Him in any other fashion.

FAMILY PRAYER TIME

For Families with Young Children:

Father, You have given our family so many nice things. We know that You expect us to help others who are in need. Give our family ideas about how we can help these people. Show us what we can do to love our neighbors this Christmas. We know that many of them don't know You. Use us to meet their needs and to tell them about why we celebrate the birth of Your Son. Amen.

For Families with Older Children:

Father, this Christmas we want to imitate the Good Samaritan who met his neighbor's need. We ask You to give our family a heart to meet the needs of our neighbors all year. Just as the Mills family was able to share the gospel with hurting people, we long to be used by You, too. We ask You to bring people into our lives who are in need this Christmas, and we ask that You would prepare their hearts to hear about the Savior in whose name we minister. Amen.

God Rest Ye Merry, Gentlemen
(Selected verses)
Author unknown

God rest ye merry, gentlemen, let nothing you dismay,
Remember Christ our Savior was born on Christmas Day;
To save us all from Satan's power when we were gone astray.

Refrain:
O tidings of comfort and joy, comfort and joy;
O tidings of comfort and joy.

In Bethlehem, in Israel, this blessèd Babe was born,
And laid within a manger upon this blessèd morn;
The which His mother Mary did nothing take in scorn. (Refrain)

From God our heavenly Father a blessèd angel came;
And unto certain shepherds brought tidings of the same;
How that in Bethlehem was born the Son of God by name.
(Refrain)

"Fear not, then," said the angel, "Let nothing you afright
This day is born a Savior of a pure Virgin bright,
To free all those who trust in Him from Satan's power and
might." (Refrain)

The shepherds at those tidings rejoiced much in mind,
And left their flocks a-feeding in tempest, storm and wind,
And went to Bethl'em straightaway this blessèd Babe to find.
(Refrain)

Now to the Lord sing praises all you within this place,
And with true love and brotherhood each other now embrace;
This holy tide of Christmas all others doth deface. (Refrain)

That God send you a happy new year, happy new year,
And God send you a happy new year.

Family Discussion Topics:

❦ How would you react if you were in the hospital during Christmas and a family you didn't know brought you cookies, gave you a gift, and shared the Christmas story with you?

❦ What new tradition could your family start this Christmas that would meet the needs of people in your community?

❦ What did Jesus mean when He said that we are to love our neighbors as ourselves?

Family Activities:

❦ Call hospitals that are close to your home to find out if your family could celebrate Christmas with some of the patients.

❦ Have each family member go through his or her things and pick out one new or like new item to give to someone in need this Christmas.

DECEMBER 10

CHRISTMAS SYMBOLS AND TRADITIONS: CHRISTMAS TREES

There shall come forth a shoot from the stump of Jesse, and a branch from his roots shall bear fruit.
ISAIAH 11:1

FAMILY DEVOTION

Decorating a Christmas tree is fun. Some families hang handmade ornaments and some add one new ornament each year. Some go all out by hanging as many ornaments and lights as will fit on the tree. When the lights on the tree are finally turned on, suddenly it feels like Christmas.

No one knows for sure who first thought of a Christmas tree, but as Christians, the tree can remind us of Jesus for several reasons. First, Jesus is called the "branch" of Jesse because He descended from a man named Jesse. Others think of the cross (sometimes referred to as a tree) that Jesus died on to atone for our sins. The cross can be traced back to Adam and Eve, who ate from the tree of the knowledge of good and evil.

This year, when you look at Christmas trees and watch their twinkling lights, think about Jesus. Only Jesus faithfully came to earth to hang on a tree so that you could live with Him forever.

GOING DEEPER

The history of the Christmas tree is far from settled. While several accounts predate the birth of Christ, and probably have merit, Christmas trees as we know them may have their origins in one of the two following scenarios—or in a mixture of the two.

One account says that St. Boniface, an eighth-century missionary in Germany, cut down an oak tree in Germany that pagans-turned-Christians used to worship. Legend has it that he then either planted a fir tree in its place, or that one spontaneously grew there. Either way, St. Boniface is said to have told the new converts to take the fir tree as a symbol of their faith because the tree pointed heavenward and the evergreen was a reminder of eternal life.

Another account says that Martin Luther, while walking near his home one winter (either after a church service or simply contemplating his next sermon), was moved by the many stars he saw that evening above the evergreen trees. Some say the light on the trees made him think about the star over Bethlehem when Jesus was born, and others say it reminded him that Jesus was the light of the world. Luther cut down an evergreen tree, took it home, and placed candles on the branches to try to recapture what he saw for his family. Because no recorded history refers to Christmas trees becoming popular in Germany until at least sixty years after Luther's death, some deny this account.

Regardless of its origin, the Christmas tree is a wonderful way to remember that Christ is the "branch" of Jesse. God was faithful to deliver the Savior through the line of Jesse, just as He said He would in Isaiah 11:1.

We should also remember that Jesus is the light of the world that shines in the darkness and calls sinners to repentance. Each light on the tree can be a symbol of Christ sending forth missionaries to bring light into the dark places of the world.

Finally, the Christmas tree can serve as a reminder about the redeeming power of Christ. When Satan tempted Adam and Eve to eat of the tree of the knowledge of good and evil, they fell into sin, and they took the rest of humankind with them. But Christ redeemed us by hanging on a tree.

FAMILY PRAYER TIME

For Families with Young Children:

Father, help us to see Jesus better every time we look at a Christmas tree. When we see the branches, remind us that Jesus is the branch of Jesse. When we see the lights, remind us that Jesus is the light of the world. When we see the tree as a whole, remind us that Jesus hung on a tree for our eternal salvation. Amen.

For Families with Older Children:

Father, we know You to be a creative God who uses even the small things of life like Christmas trees to express and point to Your glory. We see such rich biblical symbolism in Christmas trees. We marvel over Your sovereign, omnipotent ways in which You orchestrated the birth of the Branch. We praise You for shining Your light into the darkness of our world. And we fall at Your feet in reverence and gratitude for Your willingness to send Your Son to die on the tree. Amen.

Beautiful Christmas
Words by Mary B. Slade

O'er the hills and adown the snowy dells,
As the echoes ring of the Christmas bells,
Angel songs in our hearts resound again,
Singing peace on earth and good will to men!

Refrain:
Bring pine and fir tree, weave the garlands bright,
Gladden the temple of the King tonight!
Christmas is here! Fill it with cheer;
Make it glorious with joy and light.

Bring good will to the suffering and sad;
Speak the tender word that shall make them glad;
Tell them how, o'er the hills of Bethlehem
When the angels sang, 'twas good news for them. (Refrain)

Peace on earth! bid all strife and tumult cease;
For this night again gives the Lord His peace;
While our hands shall His temple beautify,
Carol, glory be unto God most high. (Refrain)

So glad hearts on this happy Christmas night
Bring your gifts of love, make His altar bright;
Sing glad songs that shall sweetly sound as when
Angels sang of peace and good will to men. (Refrain)

Family Discussion Topics:

❧ How does understanding some of the symbolism of the Christmas tree better help you to celebrate the season?

❧ Why is it important to know that Jesus is the "branch" of Jesse?

❧ In what ways is Jesus the light of the world?

Family Activities:

❧ Gather around a Christmas tree and try to find other symbols of biblical truths about the birth of Christ.

❧ Find a friend or family member who hasn't yet decorated a tree and offer to help. As you do, tell him or her about the symbolism of the Christmas tree.

DECEMBER 11

CHRISTMAS WORSHIP: MARY'S WORSHIP

But Mary treasured up all these things, pondering them in her heart.
LUKE 2:19

FAMILY DEVOTION

When you really like something, you spend time thinking about it. You think about your best friends; your favorite sport, book, or TV show; or playing a new computer game. As Christians, we should think about God and how He wants us to live.

After Jesus was born and was lying in the manger, shepherds came to visit Mary, Joseph, and Jesus.

The shepherds told Mary that they had been visited by an angel and the angel said that the Savior had been born that day in Bethlehem. They told Mary that the angel told them where to find Jesus, the newborn Messiah. Then they told Mary that many more angels appeared and began praising God.

Mary thought about all the things the shepherds told her. The verse you read today says that she "pondered them in her heart." She certainly had a lot to think about. Mary can show us how to worship Jesus during the Christmas season.

GOING DEEPER

Some Bible commentators believe that Luke had access to Mary or her written account of the events leading up to and immediately following the birth of Christ when he wrote the Gospel of Luke. They cite Mary's actions in Luke 2:19 and say that Luke wouldn't have known her deep thoughts surrounding the birth of Jesus without such access.

Whether or not Luke had access to Mary or her written records, God has given us an intimate account of what Mary experienced shortly after she delivered Jesus. First, she *treasured* all that she'd heard—starting with the words that Gabriel spoke to her (in Luke 1:26–33). Gabriel told her that she had found favor with God and that God had chosen her to deliver the Messiah. Later we read that the shepherds told her that an angel visited them to tell them that the Messiah had been born.

Second, Mary *pondered* all that she had heard. The Greek word for *pondered* in this case means to combine, consider, or compare. Mary thought through every detail surrounding the birth of her son, and she appeared to be so moved by holy wonder that she took on a spirit of worship. God was near—so near that she had just delivered God incarnate. He was active. And He chose her. How could she not be moved?

But Mary isn't the only person who should be moved by the birth of the Savior. God is always near to His people. God is always active. And He has chosen to redeem us. As your family contemplates all that God has done this Christmas season by orchestrating the birth of Christ, take some time to worship silently in holy reverence. Ponder all that He has done for you, your family and friends, and for humankind throughout the ages.

Ponder God's mercy. Ponder His grace. Ponder the idea of God taking on flesh knowing that He would one day die a brutal death for your sins. And then allow all that you are pondering to transport you to a place of Christmas worship.

For Families with Young Children:

Father, help us to be like Mary. Help us to think deeper about the birth of Christ and to love Your Son. As we think about these things, help us to worship You often in silence. Amen.

For Families with Older Children:

Father, we struggle sometimes to worship You in silence. We have so many other things running through our minds. Help us to see past the temporal so we can ponder eternity. Quiet our minds and give us a spirit of contemplative, reverent reflection about the incarnation. May You remain the focus of our attention and affection throughout the Christmas season and beyond. Amen.

Silent Night
Words by Josef Mohr

Silent night, holy night,
All is calm, all is bright
Round yon virgin mother and Child.
Holy Infant, so tender and mild,
Sleep in heavenly peace,
Sleep in heavenly peace.

Silent night, holy night,
Shepherds quake at the sight;
Glories stream from heaven afar,
Heavenly hosts sing Alleluia!
Christ the Savior is born,
Christ the Savior is born!

Silent night, holy night,
Son of God, love's pure light;
Radiant beams from Thy holy face
With the dawn of redeeming grace,
Jesus, Lord, at Thy birth,
Jesus, Lord, at Thy birth.

Silent night, holy night
Wondrous star, lend thy light;
With the angels let us sing,
Alleluia to our King;
Christ the Savior is born,
Christ the Savior is born!

Family Discussion Topics:

❧ When was the last time you worshiped God silently as Mary did in Luke 2:19?

❧ Do you think it's easier to worship God in silence? Explain.

❧ What can your family do during the Christmas season to stop all of the noise and activity long enough to worship God in silence?

Family Activities:

❧ List the reasons that you feel compelled to worship God silently this Christmas (for example, the incarnation, God sending His Son for you, God's faithfulness to orchestrate the birth of the Savior, and so on).

❧ Spend five minutes in silent prayer and worship surrounded by your family—keeping in mind all of the things on your list.

December 12

Sharing the Christmas Experience: Jesus Evangelizes

"I must preach the good news of the kingdom of God to the other towns as well; for I was sent for this purpose."
Luke 4:43

Once, Jesus entered a town called Capernaum in Galilee. As He taught in the synagogues, or the Jewish places of worship, people were amazed because He spoke as someone who knew a great deal. A demon-possessed man approached Jesus in the synagogue, and Jesus cast the demon out of him. Then Jesus healed Peter's mother-in-law, who was sick with a high fever. Soon, many sick people came to Jesus hoping to be healed.

After casting out demons and healing many people, Jesus departed to what the Bible calls "a desolate place." Jesus needed time to be alone. But still the people followed Him. They didn't want Him to leave. That's when Jesus told them that He had to preach the good news of the gospel to other towns because that was His purpose.

Jesus was in the business of sharing the Christmas experience with others because He knew it was the reason He had come to earth. And now, we can share Jesus with others.

GOING DEEPER
After being driven out of the synagogue in Nazareth because He inferred that the kingdom of God was also available to the Gentiles, Jesus found a much more accepting audience in Capernaum. (This receptive situation was only temporary—the city eventually ended up in ruins because of the people's unbelief, just as Jesus predicted in Matthew 11:23–24.)

The people of Capernaum were "astonished at his teaching, for his word possessed authority" (Luke 4:32).

No doubt they were accustomed to teachers who cited authorities. Jesus was the absolute authority, so He didn't need to quote anybody. He then displayed His authority by casting a demon out of a man right in the synagogue. Even the demon knew who Jesus was, calling Jesus "the Holy One of God" (Luke 4:34).

After leaving the synagogue, Jesus visited Simon Peter's house, where He healed his mother-in-law, who was sick with a high fever. Word about Jesus' ministry spread quickly, and soon "all those who had any who were sick with various diseases brought them to him, and he laid his hands on every one of them and healed them" (Luke 4:40).

Jesus, who started to heal the sick and cast out demons at sunset in Capernaum, spent the entire night doing so, and finally got away from the crowd the next day to "a desolate place"—surely to rest and pray. But the people found Him and tried to keep Him from leaving.

Jesus continued with the theme He spoke about in Nazareth when He responded to the people from Capernaum: "I must preach the good news of the kingdom of God to the other towns as well; for I was sent for this purpose" (Luke 4:43).

Jesus came to tell people that the kingdom of God was at hand. In a sense, He came to share the Christmas experience with as many as would listen. Thirty years had passed since His birth and a great number of people still didn't know who He was or understand why He had come. As the chief cornerstone of the church, it was His job to tell them.

Now, as the representatives of Jesus' church, it is our job to share the Christmas experience. And what a joyous event it is when people understand, for the first time, who Jesus is and why He came. Share the experience of Christmas with someone today.

FAMILY PRAYER TIME

For Families with Young Children:

Father, we know that You sent Jesus to earth to live and then die for people of every nation. Help us to tell people we don't know about Jesus. Help us to be excited to tell others this Christmas about the kingdom of God. Amen.

For Families with Older Children:

Father, we see the heart that Jesus had for the people of Galilee and beyond. We see His wisdom in knowing when to speak and when to stay silent. We see His discernment in knowing when to stay and when to leave. We see His authority, which even the demons acknowledged. Give us His heart, His wisdom, and His discernment so that we might share the Christmas experience with authority. Amen.

Join All Ye Joyful Nations
(Selected verses)
Words by Charles Wesley

Join all ye joyful nations
The acclaiming hosts of Heav'n!
This happy morn a Child is born
To us a Son is given.

The Messenger and Token
Of eternal favor,
God hath sent down to us His Son,
A universal Savior!

The wonderful Messiah,
Joy of every nation,
Jesus His Name, with God the fame,
The Lord of all creation.

The Counsellor of sinners,
Mighty to deliver,
The Prince of Peace, whole love's increase,
Shall reign in Man forever.

Go see the King of glory,
Seek the Heavenly Stranger,
So poor and mean, His court an inn,
His cradle is a manger.

Who from His father's bosom
Now for us descended
Who built the skies, on earth He lies,
By only beasts attended.

Family Discussion Topics:

❧ Why did Jesus need to leave the people in Capernaum even though they wanted Him to stay?

❧ If Jesus came to earth to tell others about the kingdom of God, how should this change the way we celebrate Christmas?

❧ Jesus knew when to speak and when to stay silent. He also knew when to stay and when to go. How can your family obtain similar wisdom and discernment when sharing the Christmas experience?

Family Activities:

❧ Plan a family trip to an area (in your city or otherwise) where you normally don't go and find a way to share the gospel there.

❧ Decide as a family to spend a certain amount of time studying the Bible each day. By doing so, you'll be able to teach others with authority and you'll be prepared to give an answer when someone asks about your faith.

December 13

The Names of the Messiah: Mighty God

For to us a child is born, to us a son is given; and the government shall be upon his shoulder, and his name shall be called Wonderful Counselor, Mighty God, Everlasting Father, Prince of Peace.
ISAIAH 9:6

Jesus upset many people when He was on earth. They couldn't understand how He claimed to be one with the Father (John 10:30), the way to the Father (John 14:6), the spokesman for the Father (John 12:49), and a reflection of the Father (John 14:9). But if they had understood what the prophet Isaiah said in today's verse long before Jesus was born, they would have known that Jesus is also called "Mighty God."

How could a baby be referred to as "Mighty God"? How could any man be referred to as "Mighty God"? Only a baby who came from heaven could deserve such a title, and only a baby who was God Himself.

That's exactly who Jesus claimed to be. Jesus is God in the form of a man. When we worship the baby Jesus at Christmas, we are worshiping the "Mighty God."

GOING DEEPER

In our postmodern culture, few seem to understand that Christmas is about much more than the celebration of a baby who was born in Bethlehem more than two thousand years ago. The birth of Jesus has become a nice story that many people hear once a year, but most don't see the relevancy of the story to their lives.

Understanding that the baby Jesus wasn't just a baby but the "Mighty God" might change their minds. Indeed, He is the same mighty God who formed the earth (Genesis 1:26), led the Israelites out of captivity in Egypt (Exodus 12:17), wrote and handed down the Ten Commandments to Moses on Mount Sinai (Deuteronomy

4:13), commanded the Israelites to conquer the land of Canaan and then went ahead of them into battle (Deuteronomy 31:3), and, finally, loved humankind enough to make the ultimate provision for the forgiveness of our sins (John 3:16).

As surely as Jesus was with God in the beginning (John 1:1), he was the "Mighty God" who did all of these things, and much more. Jesus is the creator and sustainer of all things (Colossians 1:16). He is righteous, just, pure, and without sin (2 Corinthians 5:21). He has command over the weather (Luke 8:24) and the angels (Matthew 26:53). And He is the founder and perfecter of faith (Hebrews 12:2).

Christmas is about remembering the "Mighty God" who saw fit to leave heaven, be born of a virgin, and one day to lay down His life so that we might live eternally with the Father.

Never allow yourself to think of Jesus during Christmas as merely an infant. Normal infants are born with a sin nature that demands to be appeased and that leads them far from God until they are redeemed. The Christ child never sinned, never strayed from God, and never demanded anything in a sinful fashion.

As you and your family think about the birth of the perfect child this Christmas, keep in mind that even in His infancy, Jesus was the "Mighty God." Allow that fact to stir up a holy reverence in your heart for Christ—and then marvel that the mighty God was born for you.

For Families with Young Children:

Father, help us to remember that one of the names of Jesus is "Mighty God." When we worship Jesus this Christmas, give us feelings of fear and joy. Even though You are so holy and we are so sinful, still You chose to come to earth as a baby who would grow up to die for us. Amen.

For Families with Older Children:

Father, when we think about all of Your mighty acts as recorded in Your Word, we admit that we rarely equate them with the works of Christ. Give us a more complete picture of the Christ child this Christmas. May we never view Him as being similar in nature to any other child who was ever born. For even as an infant, He was indeed the Mighty God. Amen.

For Unto Us a Child Is Born

Words by Susan H. Peterson

For unto us a child is born,
To us a son is giv'n;
The government shall rest on him,
Th' anointed One from heav'n.
His name is Wonderful Counselor,
The Mighty God is He,
The Everlasting Father,
The humble Prince of Peace.

The increase of his government
And peace shall never end;
He'll reign on David's ancient throne
As ruler of all men.
Upheld with justice and righteousness,
Forever his kingdom will last;
The zeal of the Lord God Most High
Will bring these things to pass.

Lord Jesus, come now and reign in me,
Be Lord of my life this hour.
Come be my Counselor and my God,
My source of wisdom and power.
Watch o'er me with your Father care,
My heart and my mind, fill with peace.
I worship you, my Lord and King,
My praise will never cease.

Family Discussion Topics:

❧ In what ways is Jesus the Mighty God?

❧ Does that knowledge change how you will celebrate Christmas?

❧ How would failing to understand the fullness of Jesus hinder a person's ability to worship Him properly at Christmas?

Family Activities:

❧ Listen to Handel's *Messiah* again (as we did on December 6 when we studied Jesus as Wonderful Counselor), and allow family members to worship the Mighty God however they choose.

❧ Read the following passages: John 1:1; Colossians 1:16; 2 Corinthians 5:21; Luke 8:24; Matthew 26:53; and Hebrews 12:2. Take a couple of minutes to thank God as a family for sending the Mighty God to earth.

DECEMBER 14

CHRISTMAS PRAYERS:
CONFESSION

And even if our gospel is veiled, it is veiled only to those who are perishing. In their case the god of this world has blinded the minds of the unbelievers, to keep them from seeing the light of the gospel of the glory of Christ, who is the image of God.
2 CORINTHIANS 4:3-4

Family Prayer

Father, we don't always act like we know You at Christmastime. We know the truth of the Bible, and we know You have forgiven our sins. Still, it is easy for us to find other things we would rather do than worship You. We have parties to attend, presents to buy, decorations to make, and, of course, we keep thinking about all the presents we might receive.

We're sad that we have missed chances to tell others about the true meaning of Christmas. We need to help shine the light of the gospel into their dark worlds. We know that Satan has blinded them and that only the gospel can make them fully aware of You and the salvation You offer.

Forgive us, Father, for not being solely focused on You this Christmas. Forgive us for the opportunities we've missed to share the gospel. Forgive us for being selfish. Forgive us for getting so caught up in the things of this world that we have failed to think about eternity. Help us to spend more time thinking about, praying about, and telling others about Jesus—who is the way, the truth, and the life. Amen.

Going Deeper Prayer

Father, we confess that in our desire to enjoy Christmas, we are often easily led astray. We know that You don't consider many of our Christmas activities to be sinful in and of themselves, but by our failing to do everything out of love for You, we have sinned.

We sin when our hearts, which are often full of covetousness, want more extravagant gifts when so many are without food, clothing, and shelter.

We sin when we spend so much time focused on ourselves that we fail to share the gospel with unbelievers. Now is the time when so many are more willing to listen to Your message of hope.

We sin when we strive to create the "perfect" Christmas in our homes but fail to center our environment and activities around You, the picture of perfection.

We've been too busy with the things of this world and not busy enough with the things of eternity. We know that we should spend more time as a family in Your Word and in prayer.

Forgive us, Father, for these sins, and any others that don't come readily to mind. Help us to make this a holy season, completely set apart for You and Your kingdom. Amen.

MAKING IT PERSONAL

Consider a time of silent prayer about one or more of the following:

❧ Ask God to reveal other sins you have committed during the Christmas season that steal from His glory and then ask Him to forgive you.

❧ If you are in a difficult place spiritually and you feel unable to examine your heart, confess that to God and ask for His mercy.

❧ If you need help to stay on track this Christmas, pray about finding someone to help you put James 5:16 into practice: "Confess your sins to one another and pray for one another. . . ."

- Think about one specific person in your neighborhood who is spiritually blind. Confess your lack of attempts to share the gospel with this person, and ask God to give you another opportunity this Christmas.

- Praise God for His willingness to accept your prayers of confession this Christmas season—knowing that you are not deserving of such acceptance apart from Christ.

CLOSING FAMILY PRAYER

Father, we've confessed our sins to You as a family and individually. We don't want this time we've spent with You to be for naught. We want to experience Your life-changing grace this Christmas season. Keep us close to You and don't allow us to stumble. If we do, though, be quick to remind us of our faults so we can confess them to You.

We look at our neighborhood, our city, our state, and our nation, and we are grieved over the lack of desire to worship You. People have become offended by nativity scenes. The name of Christ is spoken less often during the holiday that bears His name. And every year Christmas seems to become more consumed with material goods.

We've already confessed to being part of the problem, Father. Now we want to be part of the solution. Help our family to be so enraptured this Christmas with the virgin birth of our Messiah that we make a difference in our immediate spheres of influence. Help us to loosen the grip that the things of this world have on our hearts so that You can fill us with the wonder of Christmas. We'll be quick to give You the glory. Amen.

DECEMBER 15

FULFILLED PROPHECIES:
DESCENDED FROM THE TRIBE OF JUDAH

OLD TESTAMENT PROPHECY:

The scepter shall not depart from Judah, nor the ruler's staff from between his feet, until tribute comes to him; and to him shall be the obedience of the peoples.

GENESIS 49:10

FAMILY DEVOTION

In the Old Testament, God made a promise to Abraham: "And I will establish my covenant between me and you and your offspring after you throughout their generations for an everlasting covenant, to be God to you and to your offspring after you" (Genesis 17:7). God kept His promise to Abraham and his wife Sarah.

Abraham and Sarah had a child named Isaac, who had a child named Jacob, who had many children—one of whom was named Judah. Judah and his descendants would represent one of the twelve tribes of Israel.

Shortly before Jacob died, he called all of his sons together because he had a message he wanted to share with each of them. Part of what Jacob told Judah can be found in today's verse. Jacob told Judah that an everlasting ruler would come out of his tribe. In so doing, God continued faithfully to work out His promise with Abraham.

The Gospel of Matthew makes it clear that the everlasting ruler that Jacob spoke about was Jesus (see Matthew 1:1–17). As you celebrate Christmas this year, be grateful that you serve a God who is faithful to keep His promises. Know, too, that He's always had your salvation in mind.

GOING DEEPER

After God established what is known as the Abrahamic covenant, He often repeated His plans to Abraham.

In Genesis 15:5, God said: "Look toward heaven, and number the stars, if you are able to number them. . . So shall your offspring be." In Genesis 17:7, God said,

"And I will establish my covenant between me and you and your offspring after you throughout their generations for an everlasting covenant." In Genesis 22:17, God said, "I will surely bless you, and I will surely multiply your offspring as the stars of heaven and as the sand that is on the seashore. And your offspring shall possess the gate of his enemies. . . ."

Jacob was well aware of the promises God made to his grandfather. And as Jacob neared death, he called his sons together. He had a special message for each of them. He told Judah that "the scepter" (a symbol of kingship) would not depart from him (or his descendants). God chose Judah to carry out His promise to Abraham.

God continued to be faithful throughout the generations. God made this promise to King David, a descendant of Judah: "And your house and your kingdom shall be made sure forever before me. Your throne shall be established forever" (2 Samuel 7:16).

A time was coming when God's promise to Abraham, Judah, and David would be fulfilled to the utmost. But God's people would have to wait as God Himself orchestrated the events of history.

Matthew's Gospel (Matthew 1:1–17) describes God's faithfulness through the generations. Here we find out who God had been pointing to all along—Jesus Christ, the long-awaited Messiah, also known as "the Lion of the tribe of Judah" (Revelation 5:5), and the "King of kings and Lord of lords" (Revelation 19:16).

Remember God's promise to Abraham from Genesis 22:17? It's the one that said, "And your offspring shall possess the gate of his enemies. . . ." See if the words of Jesus, as recorded in Matthew 16:18, don't have a different, even more powerful ring to them now: "I will build my church, and the gates of hell shall not prevail against it."

As we wait in eager anticipation this Christmas season to celebrate the birth of our Savior, rejoice that we not only serve a God who is faithful, but that our Messiah has firmly established His church, and His church will triumph.

FAMILY PRAYER TIME

For Families with Young Children:
Father, thank You for Your faithfulness to believers from Adam and Eve to today. We see Your hand at work since the beginning of time, and most especially this Christmas as we celebrate the birth of Jesus our Savior. Seeing Your faithfulness makes us want to worship You even more this Christmas season. Amen.

For Families with Older Children:
Father, Your faithfulness to believers throughout the ages overwhelms us. We see Your loving hand at work long before we were born. We see that You had a plan for each generation. We see that You had a plan to redeem us before we ever realized our need for You. Much like the saints of old looked forward to the day that the Messiah would arrive on the scene, we look forward to worshiping the Lion of the tribe of Judah on Christmas Day. Amen.

The Wonder of the Story
Words by Charles I. Junkin

O the wonder of the story
Of the night so long ago,
In the glimmer of the starlight
And the whiteness of the snow,
When the little Prince of Judah
In His beauty came to birth,
While the angels sang His glory
And His sweetness filled the earth!

O the wonder of the story,
Of the gladness none can tell,
When the shepherds saw the rising
Of the Star of Israel,
And a light from out the manger,
Reaching far and waxing strong
Till it touched the darkened shadows
And the world was wrapped in song!

O the wonder of the story,
Of the tender joy supreme!
O the mystery of loving
And the sweetness of the dream!
For the little head was pillowed
On a mother's loving breast,
And the Father's little children
They shall find the perfect rest!

Family Discussion Topics:

❧ Do you tend to skip over the genealogies in the Bible? If so, why?

❧ How might genealogies help you to see God's faithfulness?

❧ How was Jesus the perfect fulfillment of the promise that God made to Abraham?

Family Activities:

❧ Read the genealogy of Jesus out loud as it is recorded in Matthew 1:1–17.

❧ Pick out a character or two (maybe Rahab or Manasseh) from the genealogy of Jesus in Matthew 1:1–17 and read his or her story. See how God uses people who sometimes go astray to glorify Himself. (For Rahab, read Joshua 2:1–21 and Hebrews 11:31; for Manasseh, read 2 Kings 21.)

DECEMBER 16

FAMILY SERVICE:
NANCY AND SUSAN

They asked us to remember the poor, the very
thing I was eager to do.
GALATIANS 2:10

FAMILY DEVOTION

Nancy and her good friend Susan came up with an idea about how to help the poor one Christmas many years ago. Together with Nancy's two children and Susan's children, the two friends drove from their small town in the state of Nebraska about twenty miles to downtown Omaha. They knew they would find people there who needed help.

They handed out hot turkey noodle soup, peanut butter and jelly sandwiches, toothpaste and soap, and tracts. Nancy said that the people they helped didn't say a lot other than "thank you," but, she said, "We could tell from their eyes that they were touched and particularly grateful for the hot turkey soup."

In today's verse Paul wanted to reach out to the poor and needy during his day, too. Paul spoke to three of Jesus' disciples, and they saw that God was with Paul in his desire to minister to the Gentiles (or non-Jewish people). They just wanted to make sure that Paul remembered the poor among the Gentiles. Like Nancy, Susan, and their children, Paul was eager to do so.

Jesus said that we will always have poor people among us (John 12:8). What better time to reach out and help them in the name of Jesus than during Christmas?

GOING DEEPER

As the gospel first began to spread to the Gentile world, the disciples learned that a great famine was about to occur (see Acts 11:27–30). Because they knew that the believers in Judea would need help, they sent relief to them via Barnabas and Saul (Paul).

God changed Saul from a murderer of believers to someone who had compassion for poor Christians. Only God could do such a thing. Paul was also burdened and called by God to reach out to the Gentile world with the gospel.

After discussion with James, Cephas (Peter), and John, the disciples "gave the right hand of fellowship" to Barnabas and Paul. But before Barnabas and Paul left, the apostles wanted to make sure that Barnabas and Paul remembered the poor when they got there (Galatians 2:10).

Paul didn't need such a reminder. He said that he was eager to remember the poor, as evidenced by his earlier relief effort to Judea.

Nancy Williams and her friend Susan Rule didn't need any such reminders either. To them Christmas seemed like the perfect time of year to meet the needs of the poor in their community. In addition to seeing the grateful glances from the needy, Nancy and Susan saw their children being transformed into people who also shared a burden for the needy.

"Our children still talk about this experience [even though it was more than fifteen years ago], remembering it with great fondness—one of those poignant memorable experiences," Nancy said.

"From what I observed, it also gave them a wider view of the world and how Jesus is pleased when we reach out to those less fortunate than we are. It was a visual demonstration of how much God had blessed both of our families and how 'there but for the grace of God, go I.' "

This Christmas your family will have many opportunities to minister to the needy in your community. Most churches and many civic groups organize such events, but you don't necessarily need to wait for them before you get involved. Nancy and Susan found a practical, tangible way to remember the poor. You can, too. Get involved and feel the joy of not only being used by God but also the joy that comes from helping others.

FAMILY PRAYER TIME

For Families with Young Children:
Father, we want to be like the apostle Paul and like Nancy, Susan, and their children. Give us a burden for the poor, and for ideas of how we can meet their needs this Christmas. We can think of no better way to celebrate the birth of Your Son than to help others in His name. Amen.

For Families with Older Children:
Father, we know that the fruit of the Spirit consists of love, joy, peace, patience, kindness, goodness, faithfulness, gentleness, and self-control. Increase our desire as a family to exhibit Your love, kindness, and gentleness to the poor in our community. We want the poor to come to know the saving power of Your Son, whose birthday we celebrate. Amen.

Hail to the Lord's Anointed
(Selected verses)
Words by James Montgomery

Hail to the Lord's anointed, great David's greater Son!
Hail in the time appointed, His reign on earth begun!
He comes to break oppression, to set the captive free;
To take away transgression and rule in equity.

He comes in succor speedy to those who suffer wrong;
To help the poor and needy, and bid the weak be strong;
To give them songs for sighing, their darkness turn to light,
Whose souls, condemned and dying, were precious in His
sight.

He shall come down like showers upon the fruitful earth;
Love, joy, and hope, like flowers, spring in His path to birth.
Before Him, on the mountains, shall peace, the herald, go,
And righteousness, in fountains, from hill to valley flow.

Kings shall fall down before Him, and gold and incense
bring;
All nations shall adore Him, His praise all people sing;
For He shall have dominion o'er river, sea and shore,
Far as the eagle's pinion or dove's light wing can soar.

For Him shall prayer unceasing and daily vows ascend;
His kingdom still increasing, a kingdom without end:
The mountain dews shall nourish a seed in weakness sown,
Whose fruit shall spread and flourish and shake like Lebanon.

O'er every foe victorious, He on His throne shall rest;
From age to age more glorious, all blessing and all blest.
The tide of time shall never His covenant remove;
His Name shall stand forever, His Name to us is Love.

Family Discussion Topics:

❧ When you hear stories about or see homeless or poor people, do you find you take your home, food, and clothing for granted?

❧ When the apostles reminded Paul to remember the poor, he said it was "the very thing" that he was eager to do. How eager are you to remember the poor?

Family Activities:

❧ Instead of baking cookies for friends at school, church, or work this year, make them for the poor who visit your local rescue mission and deliver them as a family.

❧ While you are at the rescue mission, ask about other ways your family can help.

❧ Ask friends if they know a person or a family who is struggling financially this Christmas, and then offer to help that person or family in some fashion.

December 17

Christmas Symbols and Traditions: Nativity Scenes

And she gave birth to her firstborn son and wrapped him in swaddling cloths and laid him in a manger, because there was no place for them in the inn.
Luke 2:7

FAMILY DEVOTION

Every Christmas many families look forward to setting up a nativity scene. Something about seeing a small wooden barn full of animals, wise men, shepherds, and Joseph, Mary, and the baby Jesus makes Christmas seem a little closer.

Some believe that such a tradition dates back to the thirteenth century when St. Francis of Assisi used a live nativity scene during a Christmas Eve service. By the seventeenth or eighteenth century, many wealthy people in Italy were paying to have little nativity scene figurines made for their homes.

Today, families use nativity scenes throughout the month of December to reenact the actual events of Jesus' birth. Starting with an empty stable, animals are inserted first, making sure that the wise men and the shepherds stay far away from the stable. Later, Joseph and Mary are added. Slowly everyone else is moved toward the stable. On Christmas morning, baby Jesus is placed in the manger, and the angels are put around Him—followed by the arrival of the wise men and the shepherds.

GOING DEEPER

In 1223, St. Francis of Assisi set up a live nativity in Greccio, Italy. Many accounts of the story agree that he included a manger full of straw and a borrowed donkey and ox. Some accounts say that he also included statues of Joseph, Mary, and a baby doll that represented Jesus. St. Francis is said to have been so moved while preaching at the nativity scene that night that he wasn't able to say the name of Jesus, so he referred to Him as the "Babe of Bethlehem."

Some say that St. Francis got his idea from religious leaders who went before him, but little doubt exists that people liked what he did. Soon the tradition of nativity scenes began to catch on.

By the 1300s, nativity scenes—mostly made out of wood, marble, and terracotta—began appearing in chapels in Italy. Wealthy Italian families eventually began having nativity scenes crafted for their homes. Soon the idea of nativity scenes spread into Portugal, Spain, England, and other countries.

With each passing century, nativity scenes became a little more intricate and elaborate. Today they are mass produced and readily available to most families.

No matter how fancy or scaled down the nativity scene, the thought of John 1:14 ("and the Word became flesh and dwelt among us. . .") becoming a reality ought to move us the way it moved St. Francis.

Everything changed the day Jesus was born. For centuries, Old Testament saints had been predicting and pointing toward a Messiah who would one day redeem humankind. For four hundred years in between the Old Testament and New Testament eras, God was silent. Then came news that Mary was with child and the child was indeed the long-promised Messiah.

Joseph and Mary traveled from Nazareth to Bethlehem (which is about a ninety-mile walk) when Caesar Augustus called for a census. Since the inn in Bethlehem was completely full, Mary gave birth to Jesus in a stable and placed him in a manger. Thus began the thirty-three-year earthly ministry of Jesus that eventually led to the cross.

As you enjoy your nativity scene this Christmas season, never lose sight that God Himself took on flesh and spent His first hours as a human in a manger.

FAMILY PRAYER TIME

For Families with Young Children:

Father, help us never to see the nativity scene as just a Christmas decoration. Instead, help us to see Your hand at work as You arranged all of the events of Jesus' birth. Most of all, we pray that You would use the nativity scene to remind us of the birth of our Savior, Jesus Christ. Amen.

For Families with Older Children:

Father, we know that a nativity scene is just a tool that helps to remind us about the truth found in Your Word. We pray that You would take our breath away when we gaze upon the manger this Christmas, just as you did with St. Francis of Assisi all those years ago. Amen.

O Come, All Ye Faithful
(Selected verses)
Words by John F. Wade

O come, all ye faithful, joyful and triumphant,
O come ye, O come ye, to Bethlehem.
Come and behold Him, born the King of angels;

Refrain:
O come, let us adore Him,
O come, let us adore Him,
O come, let us adore Him,
Christ the Lord.

True God of true God, Light from Light Eternal,
Lo, He shuns not the Virgin's womb;
Son of the Father, begotten, not created; (Refrain)

Sing, choirs of angels, sing in exultation;
O sing, all ye citizens of heaven above!
Glory to God, all glory in the highest; (Refrain)

Child, for us sinners poor and in the manger,
We would embrace Thee, with love and awe;
Who would not love Thee, loving us so dearly? (Refrain)

Yea, Lord, we greet Thee, born this happy morning;
Jesus, to Thee be glory given;
Word of the Father, now in flesh appearing. (Refrain)

Family Discussion Topics:

❧ Do you think that nativity scenes help or hinder family worship during Christmas?

❧ How does knowing a little bit about the history of nativity scenes help you to appreciate them more?

❧ Have you ever been moved like St. Francis of Assisi at the sight of the manger?

Family Activities:

❧ If you're using a nativity scene to reenact the birth of Christ (see the December 1 and December 8 devotions), move the wise men and the shepherds even closer than you had them before. Move Joseph and Mary closer as well. Continue to hide the angels and the baby Jesus until Christmas morning.

❧ As a family, look at the empty manger and spend a couple of minutes in private prayer, praising God for filling the manger.

DECEMBER 18

CHRISTMAS WORSHIP: ANGELS' WORSHIP

When he brings the firstborn into the world, he says, "Let all God's angels worship him."
HEBREWS 1:6

FAMILY DEVOTION

By now your family has read the Christmas story in the Gospel of Luke (chapter 2) and the Gospel of Matthew (chapters 1 and 2). You know that angels were a large part of the story—from telling Mary that she was going to have God's Son named Jesus, to praising God for the birth of Jesus.

In today's verse, God gave all of His angels a command to worship Jesus when He was born. If Jesus had been a mere man or a created being, God would not have commanded His angels to do such a thing, but since Jesus was God, the angels delighted in worshiping Him.

In Revelation 5:2–10, the apostle John records an event in heaven in which angels fall down and worship Jesus because He is the only one worthy of opening the scroll of God.

As you worship Jesus this Christmas, remember that He was more than just a baby when He was born. He was fully God and fully human. You can join with the angels in heaven who worship Him because He is worthy to be worshiped.

GOING DEEPER

When a father leaves his son an inheritance, he does so believing that his son will be faithful to use the money wisely. That doesn't always turn out to be the case, though. Sometimes, the sudden abundance of wealth is too much for people to handle.

That's not something we ever have to worry about with Jesus. He was the perfect heir—doing exactly what

His Father expected of Him. The writer of Hebrews begins by saying that God appointed Jesus to be "the heir of all things" (Hebrews 1:2). He was active in the role of Creation and "upholds the universe by the word of his power" (verse 3). He made "purification for sins" and then "sat down at the right hand of the Majesty on high, having become as much superior to angels as the name he has inherited is more excellent than theirs" (verses 3–4).

But the angels didn't worship Jesus when He was born *because* He had become superior to angels. Hebrews 2:7 says that when Jesus was born, He was a little lower than the angels—meaning He temporarily was lower because of His human form. Instead, they worshiped Him because God commanded it (Hebrews 1:6). Their worship was justified, not just because of God's command, but also because the angels became subject to Jesus even while He was here on earth.

As you think about the incarnate Son of God in the coming days, allow yourself to be overwhelmed by the fact that He is the sustainer of all things, your Redeemer, and the One who now sits at the right hand of God. Jesus loved you enough to leave perfection one glorious day over two thousand years ago.

If even the angels—who have tasted heaven and receive direct orders from God Himself—worshiped the Christ child, how much more should we do the same this Christmas? Get lost in His presence and experience Christmas in a deeper fashion than ever before.

For Families with Young Children:

Father, Your Word says that all of Your angels worshiped Jesus when He was born. As Christmas Day nears, we can hardly wait to do the same. Draw us close, Father, as we think about the day You sent Your Son from heaven to earth for us. Help us to so love worshiping Christ that we'll consider this our best Christmas ever—no matter what else happens.
Amen.

For Families with Older Children:

Father, we can hardly imagine perfection, but yet we see it in Jesus—the heir of Your kingdom and the sustainer of all things. How can we not be overwhelmed? We aren't deserving of such, but out of Your mercy and grace You sent us perfection in the form of a baby. May we never lose the wonder of that day. Amen.

Hark! The Herald Angels Sing

(Selected verses)
Words by Charles Wesley

Hark! The herald angels sing,
"Glory to the newborn King;
Peace on earth, and mercy mild,
God and sinners reconciled!"
Joyful, all ye nations rise,
Join the triumph of the skies;
With th' angelic host proclaim,
"Christ is born in Bethlehem!"

Refrain:
Hark! the herald angels sing,
"Glory to the newborn King!"

Christ, by highest Heav'n adored;
Christ the everlasting Lord;
Late in time, behold Him come,
Offspring of a virgin's womb.
Veiled in flesh the Godhead see;
Hail th' incarnate Deity,
Pleased with us in flesh to dwell,
Jesus our Emmanuel. (Refrain)

Hail the heav'nly Prince of Peace!
Hail the Sun of Righteousness!
Light and life to all He brings,
Ris'n with healing in His wings.
Mild He lays His glory by,
Born that man no more may die.
Born to raise the sons of earth,
Born to give them second birth. (Refrain)

Family Discussion Topics:

- How does the view of angels, as presented in Hebrews 1:6, differ from the one often presented in pop culture that says angels ought to be the objects of worship?

- How does this devotion give you a better understanding of the relationship between Jesus and angels?

- Even though Jesus was worthy of praise from the angels on the day He was born, how might knowing that He is the heir of all things, the upholder of the universe, and the purification for sins help you to worship Him better this Christmas?

Family Activities:

- Hebrews 1:6 says that all God's angels were instructed to worship Jesus when He was born. Spend a few minutes in silence thinking about what that must have looked like.

- Attend a Christmas play at a local church and pay extra attention to the angels as they worship Jesus.

DECEMBER 19

SHARING THE CHRISTMAS EXPERIENCE: PAUL EVANGELIZES

"And we bring you the good news that what God promised to the fathers, this he has fulfilled to us their children by raising Jesus, as also it is written in the second Psalm, 'You are my Son, today I have begotten you.'"
ACTS 13:32-33

You probably know someone who celebrates Christmas but doesn't really know the true meaning of the holiday. He knows he's celebrating the birth of Jesus, but he has no idea why Christmas is important. The apostle Paul faced similar circumstances during his first missionary journey that included a stop in a synagogue in Antioch.

The Jews in Jerusalem didn't understand that the scriptures they had been reading for many years pointed to the birth of Jesus. Paul didn't want the Jews in Antioch to make the same mistake. So, when given the opportunity to speak in the synagogue there, he quoted Psalm 2:7: "You are my Son, today I have begotten you."

Sadly, many of the Jews were jealous of the attention Paul received, and they decided to reject his message that Jesus died for their sins. But that didn't stop Paul from continuing to tell anybody who would listen that God sent His only Son to earth to pay the ultimate penalty for sin. This Christmas, be like Paul. Tell others about the Christ child.

GOING DEEPER

As a descendant of the tribe of Benjamin, the apostle Paul came from a long line of Pharisees (see Acts 23:6 and Philippians 3:5). So, when he and Barnabas stopped in a synagogue in Antioch during Paul's first missionary journey, Paul was able to remind the Jews of their history.

Paul reminded them that Israel was God's chosen people and that God had been faithful to lead them out of bondage in Egypt (Acts 13:17). After allowing Israel to wander in the desert for forty years because of the people's sinfulness, God led them to the land of Canaan, which He gave them as an inheritance (verses 18–19). God gave the Israelites judges, prophets, and, later, kings (verses 20–21). One of those kings was David.

Paul said this about David: "Of this man's offspring God has brought to Israel a Savior, Jesus, as he promised" (verse 23). But the Jews didn't understand that Jesus was the fulfillment of God's promise and they condemned Him to death on the cross (verse 27). "But God raised him from the dead" (verse 30).

Paul wanted the Jews in Antioch to know that they had another chance to embrace the Savior. Paul told them an abbreviated form of the Christmas story as found in Psalm 2:7, a passage that the Jews would have known: "You are my Son, today I have begotten you."

For a little while, the Jews in Antioch were intrigued. In the end, though, they saw Paul as more of a competitor than a preacher of truth, and they rejected him and his message.

In a sense, Paul was attempting to reach his own extended family with the gospel—one of the most difficult things to do. Sensitivities run high and personal relationships are sometimes threatened in situations like that. As much as Paul loved the Jews (at one point, he even professed that he was willing to give up his own salvation for them if they would turn to Christ—see Romans 9:3), he took the risk of offending them with the gospel.

In a spirit of love, do the same thing this Christmas. Tell people how God keeps His promises and how He loves them so much that He was willing to send His only begotten Son to earth to die for their sins.

<small>FAMILY PRAYER TIME</small>

For Families with Young Children:

Father, we are sad when we see people we know and love celebrating Christmas but not really knowing why. Help us to be gentle this Christmas when telling them about the importance of the birth of Jesus. At the same time, God, help us to be bold. Amen.

For Families with Older Children:

Father, we understand how difficult it must have been for Paul to tell the people he loved about the Savior. His people were religious and believed they were on the right course, much like many we know. Give us boldness this Christmas to clearly lay out the gospel for them the way Paul did in Acts 13. Amen.

Good Christian Men, Rejoice
Words by Heinrich Suso

Good Christian men, rejoice with heart and soul and voice;
Give ye heed to what we say: News! News! Jesus Christ is
born today;
Ox and ass before Him bow; and He is in the manger now.
Christ is born today! Christ is born today!

Good Christian men, rejoice, with heart and soul and voice;
Now ye hear of endless bliss: Joy! Joy! Jesus Christ was born
for this!
He has opened the heavenly door, and man is blest
forevermore.
Christ was born for this! Christ was born for this!

Good Christian men, rejoice, with heart and soul and voice;
Now ye need not fear the grave: Peace! Peace! Jesus Christ was
born to save!
Calls you one and calls you all, to gain His everlasting hall.
Christ was born to save! Christ was born to save!

Family Discussion Topics:

❧ Why does it seem more difficult to share the gospel with family and friends?

❧ In Romans 9:3, Paul said that he wished that he could be "cut off from Christ" for the sake of his kinsmen. How similar is your passion to reach your loved ones?

❧ What did Paul do when telling his fellow Jews the Christmas story that might help you when telling your family and friends?

Family Activities:

❧ Make a list of your unsaved friends and family members and commit to praying for a chance to share the gospel with each of them this Christmas season.

❧ Have a Christmas party in your home and invite your unsaved friends and family members. Share the gospel by reading the Christmas story from the Bible, or by using your nativity scene to retell the events of the birth of Christ.

December 20

The Names of the Messiah: Everlasting Father

For to us a child is born, to us a son is given; and the government shall be upon his shoulder, and his name shall be called Wonderful Counselor, Mighty God, Everlasting Father, Prince of Peace.
ISAIAH 9:6

FAMILY DEVOTION

We think a lot about the baby Jesus during Christmas. But Jesus was so much more than a baby. One of the names that Isaiah used when referring to the coming Messiah was "Everlasting Father." The name itself means that the Messiah has always existed and that He is God.

The Bible tells us that only one God exists—but He exists as God the Father, God the Son, and God the Holy Spirit. Each has a separate role to play, but each one is fully God. God didn't hide that fact in the Old Testament.

Through the book of Isaiah, God told His people that God the Son would come to earth one day in the form of a baby. God said that while the Messiah would be fully human, He would also be fully God—the Everlasting Father in the flesh.

As you look at the baby Jesus in a nativity set or as pictured on Christmas cards, keep in mind that you are adoring much more than a cute little baby. Jesus is worthy of our worship because He is indeed the Everlasting Father from on high.

GOING DEEPER

Nothing infuriated the Pharisees more about Jesus than when He answered their questions by claiming His deity. In one such exchange in John 8:58, Jesus told them, "Truly, truly, I say to you, before Abraham was, I am." At that, the Pharisees wanted to stone Jesus for blasphemy. They remembered that God referred to Himself in the Old Testament in the same fashion (when Moses faced his own religious scoffers). In Exodus 3:14, God said to

Moses, "I AM WHO I AM." God also told Moses to tell the people that "I AM has sent me to you."

Just as the Pharisees knew Exodus 3:14, they surely knew such scriptures as Isaiah 9:6, which referred to the coming Messiah as the "Everlasting Father." Their spiritual blindness didn't help their cause against Jesus, but neither did their willful intent to simply overlook parts of the Old Testament that clearly spoke about the deity of Christ.

Jesus didn't back down from the Pharisees, or anybody else who didn't see His deity. In the Book of Revelation (22:13), Jesus confirmed His status as the Everlasting Father: "I am the Alpha and the Omega, the first and the last, the beginning and the end." This was a reference to what God said about Himself in Isaiah 41:4: "I, the LORD, the first, and with the last; I am he."

Jesus didn't attain deity status. He was always God—even as a baby. The shepherds knew it. The wise men knew it. Joseph and Mary knew it, too. At just the right moment in history, the Everlasting Father came to earth in the form of a baby. And while He was rejected by man, first by King Herod and then by the Pharisees, He nonetheless continued living out His God-directed purpose here on earth.

As you gaze upon the likeness of the Christ child this Christmas, do so with a reverent heart, always being aware that this was no ordinary baby. Jesus, the Everlasting Father, loved you enough to make the ultimate sacrifice for your sins.

For Families with Young Children:

Father, help us to worship Jesus properly this Christmas season. We know Him to be fully God, even though He was also fully human while He was here on earth. We thank You for sending the Everlasting Father to earth. Without Him, we would have no way to pay for our sins. Amen.

For Families with Older Children:

Father, we reverently believe that Jesus was, is, and always will be the Everlasting Father, the first and the last, the Alpha and the Omega, the beginning and the end. With a sense of awe this Christmas, we worship the baby Jesus who was both fully human and fully God. Amen.

For Unto Us a Child Is Born
Words by Susan H. Peterson

For unto us a child is born,
To us a son is giv'n;
The government shall rest on him,
Th' anointed One from heav'n.
His name is Wonderful Counselor,
The Mighty God is He,
The Everlasting Father,
The humble Prince of Peace.

The increase of his government
And peace shall never end;
He'll reign on David's ancient throne
As ruler of all men.
Upheld with justice and righteousness,
Forever his kingdom will last;
The zeal of the Lord God Most High
Will bring these things to pass.

Lord Jesus, come now and reign in me,
Be Lord of my life this hour.
Come be my Counselor and my God,
My source of wisdom and power.
Watch o'er me with your Father care,
My heart and my mind, fill with peace.
I worship you, my Lord and King,
My praise will never cease.

Family Discussion Topics:

❧ How can Jesus be both God the Son and the Everlasting Father at the same time?

❧ Can you fathom what it means to have always existed?

❧ How should remembering that Jesus is the Everlasting Father change the way you celebrate Christmas?

Family Activities:

❧ Listen to Handel's *Messiah* again (as we did on December 6 and December 13 when we studied the idea of Jesus being the Wonderful Counselor and the Mighty God), and allow family members to worship the Everlasting Father however they choose.

❧ Read Revelation 22 out loud and allow yourself to be swept away in a spirit of worship of the Alpha and the Omega.

DECEMBER 21

CHRISTMAS PRAYERS:
THANKSGIVING

*And King Solomon and all the congregation
of Israel, who had assembled before him, were
before the ark, sacrificing so many sheep and oxen
that they could not be counted or numbered. . .and
it was the duty of the trumpeters and singers to
make themselves heard in unison in praise and
thanksgiving to the Lord.*
2 CHRONICLES 5:6, 13

Father, we know that You demanded the blood of animals in the Old Testament to atone for the sins of Your
people. During one such ceremony, so many sheep and
oxen were sacrificed that they couldn't be numbered.
Your people then joined together in praise and thanksgiving because You were faithful to make a way for them
to find forgiveness for their sins.

We know that You had a plan from the foundation
of the world to send Your only Son to earth to make the
final sacrifice. Just like the people in today's verse, we
praise and thank You for sending Jesus to earth. We know
that we don't deserve such mercy and grace.

We praise You for honoring Your covenant with Abraham. We praise You for the miraculous birth of Jesus. We
praise You for keeping Your protective hand upon Him.
And we praise You for the unbelievable opportunity you've
given us in Christ to be called Your children. Amen.

GOING DEEPER PRAYER

Father, we see in Your Word that as the Israelites prepared to move the ark of the covenant into the newly
constructed temple built by Solomon, they sacrificed so
many sheep and oxen that "they could not be counted or
numbered" because of Your demand for holiness.

The trumpeters and singers broke out in praise and
thanksgiving at the completion of the temple, and ultimately, because You made a way for them to be cleansed
from their sins. You arrived on the wings of their praise—
so much so "that the priests could not stand to minister

because of the cloud."

If the people of the old covenant could have such joy in their praise for You, how much more ought we to praise and thank You for sending the ultimate sacrifice in the form of Your Son. If You showed up on the wings of praise in the Old Testament, how much more will You show up today after Jesus has satisfied Your holy demands once and forever?

We thank You for sending the One who knew no sin to a world full of sin. We praise You for being willing to make a sacrifice that we were incapable of making. We praise You for honoring Your promises to the saints of old to send a Savior. And we praise You for opening our eyes so that we could know Him intimately. Amen.

MAKING IT PERSONAL

Just as the trumpeters and singers praised God out loud in unison, you can thank and praise Him about one or more of the following:

- Praise God for establishing a plan to redeem humankind.

- Thank God for being faithful to keep His promises to Abraham, Judah, and David to bring the Messiah through their bloodlines.

- Praise God for blessing His people with His presence.

- Thank God for orchestrating the events of the virgin birth and for making sure that it was recorded in the gospels so that we can relive the Christmas story.

❧ Praise God for sending His Son—even though He knew that Jesus would die a brutal death.

❧ Thank God for replacing the Old Testament system of sacrifice with the Lamb of God who takes away the sins of the world.

CLOSING FAMILY PRAYER

Father, with Christmas just four days away, we want to experience Your presence in a new and fresh way. As we continue to attend more social gatherings, we ask that You would keep us in a place where we are more desirous of praising You than anything else.

As You showed up for Israel when they praised you, we invite You into our home right now. We honor and adore You for who You are and what You've done for us.

You sent us a baby who not only redeemed us, but who became known as the King of kings and Lord of lords. Jesus is the Alpha and Omega, the beginning and the end. Apart from Him, salvation is not possible, but through Him, all things are possible.

You have been faithful through the ages. Your ways are perfect. Your name is above every other name. One day Jesus will hand back to You the keys of the kingdom and proclaim that His work on earth is done.

Most glorious, merciful Father, we bow in worship before You this Christmas season. You alone are God and we are Your people—a grateful people who never want to forget the wonder of the virgin birth of Your Son Jesus Christ. Amen.

DECEMBER 22

FULFILLED PROPHECIES:
THE MESSIAH BORN AT EXACT TIME

OLD TESTAMENT PROPHECY:

*"Know therefore and understand that from
the going out of the word to restore and build
Jerusalem to the coming of an anointed one, a
prince, there shall be seven weeks. Then for sixty-
two weeks it shall be built again with squares
and moat, but in a troubled time."*

DANIEL 9:25

FAMILY DEVOTION

One day in Babylon while Daniel was praying and confessing the sins of Israel, an angel named Gabriel appeared to him. Gabriel wanted him to know that God's people would not always be held captive. Gabriel told Daniel that an "anointed one" or a "prince" would come at the exact time God chose to save His people.

We're told in the New Testament that this anointed one has already come. Jesus appeared in the form of a baby just when Gabriel said he would. Galatians 4:4–5 says, "But when the fullness of time had come, God sent forth his Son, born of woman, born under the law, to redeem those who were under the law, so that we might receive adoption as sons."

As you look forward to Christmas Day, be encouraged that your Messiah was born at the exact moment in time when God said He would. God was, is, and always will be in control. He keeps every promise He makes!

GOING DEEPER

After Daniel was captured during one of King Nebuchadnezzar's advances against Jerusalem between 605 and 586 BC, he served the king in Babylon for many years by interpreting his dreams. After King Nebuchadnezzar's death in 562 BC, Belshazzar assumed the throne. Daniel warned the new king that he had not humbled his heart but instead "lifted [it] up. . .against the Lord of heaven" (Daniel 5:22–23). Belshazzar was slain that very night in 539 BC, and Darius the Mede became the king.

In Darius's first year as king, Daniel confessed the

sins of Israel to God (see Daniel 9:1–19). Daniel asked God to turn His anger away from Israel. Daniel desperately wanted to see God restore His people. As he prayed, Gabriel visited him and declared the following: "Seventy weeks are decreed about your people and your holy city, to finish the transgression, to put an end to sin, and to atone for iniquity, to bring in everlasting righteousness, to seal both vision and prophet, and to anoint a most holy place. Know therefore and understand that from the going out of the word to restore and build Jerusalem to the coming of an anointed one. . ." (Daniel 9:24–25).

Many Bible scholars view the "seventy weeks" as a representation of 490 years. After that, multiple views exist about where those years fit in the course of church history. One thing, however, is not disputed: God ordained a specific time in history in which He would send the "anointed one" to redeem His people.

New Testament passages like Galatians 4:4 and Ephesians 1:10 tell us that the "fullness of time" came with the birth of Jesus. In God's perfect timing, Jesus was born at precisely the moment God intended.

While Daniel looked forward to such a day, in a sense, we look backward to the day in which Christ was born. Then again, since the church began setting aside time each year to remember the birth of our Savior, we look forward to Christ's birth, knowing that God's ways and timing are perfect. For the next few days leading up to Christmas, rejoice that the anointed one has come.

For Families with Young Children:

Father, we love reading the Bible because all Your words are true. We thank You for honoring Your promises. Reading Daniel's words, and then seeing those words come true when Jesus was born, strengthens our faith and makes us look forward to Christmas Day even more. Amen.

For Families with Older Children:

Father, we see the many details You've provided for us in the Book of Daniel about Israel's history and Your plan to redeem not only Israel but the Gentiles, as well. We marvel at Your preciseness. The anointed one that Daniel spoke about has come and our anticipation about the blessed day in which we celebrate His birth continues to build. Thank You for Your faithfulness to Your saints throughout the ages. Amen.

A Song and a Carol for Christmastide

(Selected verses)
Words by George P. Grantham

A song and a carol for Christmastide
Of the Prince of the Golden Shore,
Whom armies of light, in their vesture bright,
Love, serve, and adore evermore.
Far, far below, where the sunbeams glow
On a realm of His wide domain,
Sad ruin and woe, hath come through His foe,
With trouble and sorrow and pain.

And sad is the sighing when death's dark wings
Over Paradise darkly loom;
And dark the despair of the lost ones there,
Awaiting their last fatal doom.
When thus spake the Prince to His Father dear—
"Now life with a life I will buy,
Bring help from above for the sons of My love,
For them I will suffer and die!"

Away and away to the far off land,
When the fullness of time was come,
Now speedeth the Lord of the Golden Strand
From His fair everlasting home.
So down below, and unstained by sin,
In a manger born will He be;
Thereby a lost world He did enter in,
To set the loved captives free!

Family Discussion Topics:

❧ Have you ever thought about the connection between Gabriel's words in Daniel 9:25 and the perfect timing in which God brought the birth of Christ to pass?

❧ How might thinking about this help you to see God's faithfulness and increase your joy this Christmas?

❧ How does seeing God's faithfulness in action increase your desire to be faithful to Him?

Family Activities:

❧ Read Galatians 4:1–4 and Ephesians 1:7–10 aloud.

❧ Gather together as a family in a small circle, holding hands if you like, and take turns praying prayers of thanksgiving for God sending His Son precisely when He said He would.

DECEMBER 23

FAMILY SERVICE:
THE WILLIAMS FAMILY

Thus, when you give to the needy, sound no trumpet before you, as the hypocrites do in the synagogues and in the streets, that they may be praised by others. . . .
MATTHEW 6:2

FAMILY DEVOTION

Timothy and Carla Williams wanted their family to do something for those in need at Christmas. After studying Bible passages, they decided on something called "gleaning." You might remember from the story of Ruth that gleaning was when extra grain was left in a field for the poor to collect and eat.

While Timothy and Carla couldn't leave grain in a field, Timothy did come up with the idea of "poor boxes"—or a place where the Williams family could collect all of their spare change to give to the poor. Also, as a family, they decided to stop exchanging gifts.

The idea quickly caught on at Timothy's church (where he is the pastor), and soon it became a tradition. Once a year, during Christmas, families who participate bring their poor boxes, and the children dump the change into one big bucket. Families are not allowed to count the money because Timothy and Carla don't want people to compare their gleanings.

Once the collection is taken, the church prays about what to do with the offering. Over the years the money has gone to support missionaries, prison ministries, Bibles to Nigeria, orphans, and many other worthy projects.

GOING DEEPER

Jesus was never afraid to challenge people's motivations. In Matthew 6:2, which is a small portion of Jesus' Sermon on the Mount, Jesus took on the "hypocrites" in the synagogues and the streets who were more concerned with people *seeing* their efforts to help the poor than they were with actually *helping* the poor.

Jesus said that their loss would be great. In Matthew 6:1, He said, "Beware of practicing your righteousness before other people in order to be seen by them, for then you will have no reward from your Father who is in heaven."

The Williams family wanted to find a way to help the poor without anyone knowing how much they gave. For them, Christmas was the perfect time to live out their desire to help the poor.

"When our kids were very young, we realized that we wanted to teach them to 'pick up their crosses' and that it was more blessed to give than to receive," Carla said.

Timothy and Carla decided to stop exchanging gifts as a family and start a new tradition of collecting spare change (and money from other sources such as rebates) for their "poor box" that would eventually be combined with other poor boxes at church. Because they want to be faithful to Matthew 6:2, Timothy and Carla Williams ask people not to count how much they donate.

After the church pools their money each Christmas and decides where to send it, they immediately begin thinking about the next offering.

"Kids and adults make new poor boxes for the next year," Carla said. "We cover boxes with bright paper, pictures, stickers, and scriptures. The singles especially enjoy this time since they get to work closely with the kids."

Carla said that the offerings are not always large but that they go a long way because they are given with so much love.

Even though Timothy and Carla's children are grown

and starting their own families, they plan to continue the practice with their own children.

FAMILY PRAYER TIME

For Families with Young Children:
Father, we want to put Jesus' words from Matthew 6:2 into practice. We want to give to the needy while at the same time not drawing attention to ourselves. Give us ideas as a family about how we can do that this Christmas and throughout the year. Amen.

For Families with Older Children:
Father, we pray that You will never need to call us hypocrites, as Jesus called those in the synagogues, for giving to the needy in public so we can be praised for our own efforts. We know such efforts to be in vain. Give us a pure heart and a deep desire to help the needy this Christmas and throughout the year. Amen.

O How Shall I Keep My Christmas?

(Selected verses)

Words by John Westall

"O how shall I keep my Christmas?"
My heart whispered softly to me,
For I had been reading the story
Of the Lord's nativity;
And slowly and clearly before me
The words like pictures rise,
And the scenes appear in the beauty
Of the starry Syrian skies.

O cradled He was in a manger!
For lowly and poor was He,
Whose throne is the splendors of heaven
Whose pow'r is infinity;
And He bore His cross to save us,
To save us from death and sin,
And He trod all alone the winepress
To make us pure and clean.

"O how shall I keep my Christmas?"
As they keep it in heaven above;
O keep it with peace and thanksgiving,
And kindliest deed of love;
And share with the poor and needy
The joys which the Lord gives thee;
And thy heart shall keep with the angels
The Lord's nativity.

Family Discussion Topics:

❧ What was your first thought when you heard about the Williams family's decision to stop exchanging gifts so they could give more to the poor?

❧ What do you think about their rule that families can't count their change before pouring it into a big bucket?

❧ Has this devotion generated any ideas about how your family could help people in need this Christmas?

Family Activities:

❧ Start saving your own spare change as a family to donate to a good cause at Christmas. Make sure you don't tell anybody what your family is doing or how much you've given.

❧ Start a "poor box" program at your own church—allowing each family to decide if they want to participate without heaping any guilt upon those who do not.

DECEMBER 24

CHRISTMAS SYMBOLS AND TRADITIONS: CHRISTMAS CAROLS

Let the word of Christ dwell in you richly, teaching and admonishing one another in all wisdom, singing psalms and hymns and spiritual songs, with thankfulness in your hearts to God.
COLOSSIANS 3:16

FAMILY DEVOTION

Years ago at Christmas, you never knew when you might open the front door and find a group of neighbors huddled on the porch or steps singing carols. Sometimes you could even hear them singing one or two houses down the street. That always caused the excitement to grow as they got closer to your house.

The tradition of caroling is often traced back to St. Francis of Assisi during the thirteenth century. He combined the singing of songs about the birth of Christ with a live nativity scene to help Christians see how special the season was.

The scriptures tell us that singing songs to each other is a good way to let Jesus Christ fill our hearts. Many of the Christmas carols we sing each year have Bible passages in them, which give songs the power to touch our hearts and move us into a spirit of worship.

Even though caroling from door to door isn't done so much anymore, we can still encourage one another by setting aside time to sing Christmas carols.

GOING DEEPER

God often chooses to manifest Himself to His people when they sing songs of praise.

Consider Paul and Silas, who had been thrown into a Philippian jail for preaching the gospel and casting out demons. Around midnight, with their legs in chains, they began to pray and sing hymns. Scripture says, "Suddenly there was a great earthquake, so that the foundations of the prison were shaken. And immediately all the doors were opened, and everyone's bonds were unfastened" (Acts 16:26). When their jailer saw what had happened and that the prisoners had not run away, he and his entire household became Christians.

Yes, God moves when His people praise Him. And He's always honored by truth, grounded in His Word, in musical format.

That's why Paul admonished believers to sing "psalms and hymns and spiritual songs" to one another. That's also why St. Francis of Assisi introduced the idea of singing Christmas carols around a live nativity scene.

Despite those efforts, however, the church hasn't always enjoyed such songs to celebrate the Christmas season. By the seventeenth century, in both America and Europe, many believed that since the scriptures didn't mandate the commemoration of the birth of Christ during worship that the church should not celebrate it in any form—including Christmas carols.

A number of writings in the nineteenth century, including the novel *A Christmas Carol* by Charles Dickens, helped sway public opinion and spark a new interest in both Christmas and in caroling.

Caroling provides a great opportunity to sing about our Savior to an unbelieving world. And, as evidenced in Acts 16 and Colossians 3, God uses good music that is rooted in His Word to strengthen, inform, and encourage His people.

Whether you join a group of carolers who go door-to-door or just sing carols in your own home, consider making carols part of your Christmas tradition. You'll experience Christmas in a deeper fashion than you have before.

FAMILY PRAYER TIME

For Families with Young Children:

Father, we see in Your Word that You move when your people praise You. We want to experience the joy that Paul and Silas felt in that Philippian jail as they sang spiritual songs. And we want to encourage other Christians with music that glorifies You. Help us as we sing such songs this Christmas. Amen.

For Families with Older Children:

Father, thank You for the rich heritage we have of music that honors and glorifies You. We especially thank You for Christmas carols that cause us to think deeply about Your incarnation. Use the truths found in these songs not only to bring honor to Your name in heaven but also here on earth. Amen.

I Am So Glad Each Christmas Eve

(Selected verses)
Words by Inger M. Wexelsen

I am so glad each Christmas Eve,
The night of Jesus' birth!
Then like the sun the Star shone forth,
And angels sang on earth.

The little Child in Bethlehem,
He was a King indeed!
For He came down from Heaven above
To help a world in need.

He dwells again in heaven's realm,
The Son of God today;
And still He loves His little ones
And hears them when they pray.

I am so glad on Christmas Eve!
His praises then I sing;
He opens then for every child
The palace of the King.

When mother trims the Christmas tree
Which fills the room with light,
She tells me of the wondrous Star
That made the dark world bright.

And so I love each Christmas Eve
And I love Jesus, too;
And that He loves me every day
I know so well is true.

Family Discussion Topics:

🍂 How can singing Christmas carols help you to experience the Christmas season more fully?

🍂 What is the correlation between the songs of praise that Paul and Silas sang in the Philippian jail in Acts 16 and the way God responded?

🍂 How have singing psalms and hymns and spiritual songs to fellow believers encouraged you in the past?

Family Activities:

🍂 Purchase a book of Christmas carols to use this Christmas season and for many to come.

🍂 Find a copy of *A Christmas Carol* by Charles Dickens and read it together as a family.

DECEMBER 25

CHRISTMAS WORSHIP: SIMEON'S WORSHIP

When the parents brought in the child Jesus...
he [Simeon] took him up in his arms and
blessed God and said, "Lord, now you are letting
your servant depart in peace, according to your
word; for my eyes have seen your salvation..."
LUKE 2:27-30

FAMILY DEVOTION

When Jesus was born, a faithful man of God named Simeon lived in Jerusalem. The Holy Spirit promised him that he would not die before he saw the Messiah. The Holy Spirit guided Simeon to the temple in Jerusalem when Joseph and Mary brought Jesus to present Him to the Lord.

When Simeon saw the baby Jesus, he picked Him up and blessed God. God had been faithful to him by allowing him to see the Messiah. We don't know if Simeon died shortly after seeing Jesus, but we do know that Simeon's worship made him so content that he said he could die in peace.

Simeon knew that Jesus would grow up to become a light to people all over the world who live in spiritual darkness.

Today is Christmas. As you think about how Jesus came to earth to save humankind, you, too, can worship the Christ child as Simeon did more than two thousand years ago.

GOING DEEPER

We don't know a lot about Simeon from Luke 2. We know that he "was righteous and devout, waiting for the consolation of Israel, and the Holy Spirit was upon him" (Luke 2:25). We know, too, that the Holy Spirit revealed to Simeon that he would not see death until he had seen the Messiah. Beyond that, we're in the dark.

Bible commentator Adam Clarke points out that many people in Jerusalem were named Simeon, but no other man like this one particular Simeon "merited the attention of God so much as he." He also says that learned men believe that the Simeon of Luke 2 was the son of Hillel, one of the most celebrated doctors and philosophers since Moses, and the one-time president of the Sanhedrin. According to Clarke, Simeon is also said to have followed in his father's footsteps in becoming the president of the Sanhedrin. Another commentator, Matthew Henry, points to Jewish writers who came to the same conclusions.

Regardless of whether the Simeon of Luke 2 was the son of Hillel, we know that the Simeon in this passage found favor with God.

When the Holy Spirit led him to the temple where Jesus was presented to the Lord, as was the custom, Simeon took Jesus into his arms and blessed God. Imagine how Simeon must have felt. Of all the people who were alive at the time, Simeon was chosen by God to see the Christ child. Not only did he get to see Jesus, but he also got to hold Him—and in so doing, he showed us a little bit of what Christmas worship ought to look like.

Simeon didn't care whether he lived or died after being in the presence of Jesus. He was so moved by the privilege that he felt as if his life were complete. And it was. So, how could he not worship?

This Christmas Day, you, too, have the privilege of being in the presence of Jesus. When Jesus climbed the hill at Calvary to die on a cross, the curtain in the temple was torn in two from top to bottom. That act gave you and every other Christian complete access to the thrice-holy God.

Worship Him. Adore Him. Get lost in His presence. The Christ child is born this Christmas Day!

FAMILY PRAYER TIME

For Families with Young Children:
Father, we rejoice this day, much like Simeon did when he saw the baby Jesus all those years ago. While we can never be good enough to enter heaven, we know that Jesus, who was not born with a sin nature and lived a perfect life, died on the cross so that we could spend eternity with You. How could we not worship You for showing us such love? Amen.

For Families with Older Children:
Father, as much of a privilege as it was for Simeon to see the Christ child before he died, we recognize that we, too, have been blessed beyond measure because we have complete access to Jesus. Allow us to worship You today as Simeon did—the man who found such contentment in the presence of Christ that he was ready to die in peace. Amen.

Thou Light of Gentile Nations
Words by Johann Franck

Thou Light of Gentile nations, Thou Savior from above,
Drawn by Thy Spirit's leading, we come with joy and love
Into Thy holy temple and wait with earnest mind
As Simeon once had waited His God and Lord to find.

Yea, Lord, Thy servants meet Thee in every holy place
Where Thy true Word has promised that we should see Thy
face.
Today Thou still dost grant us who gather around Thee here
In arms of faith to bear Thee as did that agèd seer.

Be Thou our Joy and Brightness, our Cheer in pain and loss,
Our Sun in darkest terror, the Glory round our cross,
A Star for sinking spirits, a Beacon in distress,
Physician, Friend in sickness, in death our Happiness.

Let us, O Lord, be faithful like Simeon to the end,
So that his prayer exultant may from our hearts ascend:
"O Lord, now let Thy servant depart in peace, I pray,
Since I have seen my Savior and here beheld His day."

My Savior, I behold Thee with faith's enlightened eye;
Of Thee no foe can rob me, his threats I can defy.
Within Thy heart abiding, as Thou, O Lord, in me,
Death can no longer frighten nor part my soul from Thee.

Lord, here on earth Thou seemest at times to frown on me,
And through my tears I often can scarce distinguish Thee;
But in the heavenly mansions shall nothing dim my sight;
There shall I see Thy glory in never-changing light.

Family Discussion Topics:

❧ Why was Simeon able to believe God's promise that he would not die before seeing the Messiah?

❧ Simeon could hardly contain himself in his desire to worship. Do you feel that way this Christmas? Why?

❧ Simeon was ready to die after seeing the Savior. Do you have such peace and contentment in your life? Why?

Family Activities:

❧ If you're using a nativity scene to reenact the birth of Christ (see the devotions from December 1, 8, and 17), move Mary and Joseph and the angels into the stable. Then put Jesus in the manger, followed by the wise men and the shepherds.

❧ As a family, spend a couple of minutes in worship (either privately or openly) as you gaze upon the manger that now contains the baby Jesus.

DECEMBER 26

SHARING THE CHRISTMAS EXPERIENCE: PAUL'S EXHORTATION

But how are they to call on him in whom they have not believed? And how are they to believe in him of whom they have never heard? And how are they to hear without someone preaching?

ROMANS 10:14

You've probably noticed that people celebrate Christmas in many different ways. You've also probably noticed that some people choose not to celebrate it at all. In fact, many people have never even heard the good news of the gospel—that Jesus came to earth, lived a perfect, sinless life, suffered and died for sinners, and then rose from the dead, showing that His power is stronger than death.

But as the apostle Paul asked in today's verse, how are people supposed to believe in Jesus if they have never heard of Him? And how are they supposed to hear about Him if nobody tells them?

Just as Paul challenged the believers in Rome to tell others about Jesus, his words call us to do the same. Christmas decorations are still up. Christmas music is still playing in restaurants, shopping malls, and on the radio. And most people are still in the Christmas spirit. Today is a great day to tell people about Jesus.

GOING DEEPER

Paul wrote the letter to the Romans approximately twenty years after Jesus ascended into heaven. Amazingly, in that short time, the gospel was already beginning to unite Jews and Gentiles. The church in Rome was, in fact, composed of both.

We don't know who established the church in Rome, but we do know that Paul desperately wanted to visit once it was established. For some reason, he was unable to, saying that he was hindered many times (Romans 1:13). Surely, he wanted to make sure that they were teaching sound doctrine and to encourage them in their faith—of which the whole world was speaking (Romans 1:8).

But since he wasn't sure when he'd be able to visit, he wrote the epistle instead. While making the gospel easy to understand, he also made a point to tell the church in Rome that Israel needed the gospel just as much as the Gentiles. So he exhorted believers in Rome to tell others—both Jew and Gentile—about Christ.

The message he wanted them to share with others was simple, yet, as those in the congregation had experienced, life changing: "If you confess with your mouth that Jesus is Lord and believe in your heart that God raised him from the dead, you will be saved" (Romans 10:9).

This Christmas, you've spent a lot of time thinking about the baby Jesus and what His birth means to your life. That's a wonderful way to celebrate the season. But, as you know, even on the day in which Jesus was born, He was more than just a baby. He was the anointed One from on high. He was the Lord.

As the Christmas season begins to wind down, look for opportunities to tell others that Jesus is more than a baby who was born two thousand years ago. "For 'everyone who calls on the name of the Lord will be saved'" (Romans 10:13).

Just as the gospel brought Jew and Gentiles together in Rome all those years ago, it brings people together today from all nations and ethnic groups. Our job is to go and tell the world that our Savior has come and that He provides forgiveness for sins.

For Families with Young Children:

Father, we know people who have never really heard the gospel before. They may know about Jesus, and some even celebrate Christmas. But they don't really know Jesus because they've never called upon Him to save them from their sins. Give us a chance this week to tell at least one person about the saving power of Jesus. Amen.

For Families with Older Children:

Father, we know the power of the gospel. We see what it did in the church in Rome, and we know that it has transformed our own lives. But we know so many people who have never placed their faith in Christ, and it grieves us. We ask You to give us opportunities this coming week to tell others about the real meaning of Christmas. Amen.

From Heaven Above to Earth I Come
(Selected verses)
Words by Martin Luther

From Heaven above to earth I come,
To bear good news to every home;
Glad tidings of great joy I bring,
Whereof I now will say and sing.

To you, this night, is born a Child
Of Mary, chosen mother mild;
This tender Child of lowly birth,
Shall be the joy of all your earth.

'Tis Christ our God, Who far on high
Had heard your sad and bitter cry;
Himself will your Salvation be,
Himself from sin will make you free.

He brings those blessings long ago
Prepared by God for all below;
That in His heavenly kingdom blest
You may with us forever rest.

These are the tokens ye shall mark,
The swaddling clothes and manger dark;
There shall ye find the young Child laid,
By Whom the heavens and earth were made.

Glory to God in highest Heaven,
Who unto man His Son hath given,
While angels sing, with pious mirth,
A glad New Year to all the earth.

Family Discussion Topics:

❧ When you see unbelievers celebrating Christmas, do you normally talk to them about the reason you celebrate the season? Explain.

❧ Why does our culture no longer understand the real meaning of Christmas?

❧ What does your family do to make sure that people hear the gospel? (Do you support missionaries? Take short-term mission trips?)

Family Activities:

❧ If your family isn't already doing so, ask your pastor about a missionary family you can support (both in prayer and financially), and then share in their joy as they tell people about Jesus.

❧ Write a letter to the editor of your newspaper in which you comment about the positive aspects of the Christmas season (as they relate to the real meaning of the holiday) by complimenting a department store or business for displaying a nativity scene, and so on.

DECEMBER 27

THE NAMES OF THE MESSIAH:
PRINCE OF PEACE

*For to us a child is born, to us a son is given; and
the government shall be upon his shoulder, and
his name shall be called Wonderful Counselor,
Mighty God, Everlasting Father,
Prince of Peace.*
ISAIAH 9:6

FAMILY DEVOTION

The life and death of Jesus changed everything. Before Jesus came to earth, people like us didn't have direct access to God except when God chose to reveal Himself. And people rarely felt at peace with God. But in today's verse, Isaiah said that a day was coming when Jesus would be called the "Prince of Peace." The New Testament clearly states that Jesus was everything Isaiah predicted.

When Jesus was telling His disciples about the Holy Spirit that He would send once He was in heaven, He said, "I have said these things to you, that in me you may have peace. In the world you will have tribulation. But take heart; I have overcome the world" (John 16:33).

The apostle Paul wrote, "Therefore, since we have been justified by faith, we have peace with God through our Lord Jesus Christ" (Romans 5:1). We can't please God through our own efforts because we're all sinners and God demands death as payment for sin. But He loved us so much that He sent His Son to earth to die for our sin and to make peace with us. And in so doing, Jesus became the Prince of Peace.

GOING DEEPER

Most people spend their entire lives looking for peace. We do everything we can to attain it in relationships, at social gatherings, and in our homes, places of work, and schools. We try appeasement. We try being nice. We try being rational. And when our methods fail, we throw up our hands in the air and come to the conclusion that peace isn't possible.

Finding peace in our souls seems to be even more difficult. We look for it through good works or escapism (television, books, or shopping), or even in the spiritual disciplines of prayer, fasting, and Bible study. But still peace continues to elude us.

Our best efforts to find peace will always fail. Peace can only be found in Jesus Christ as we experience His presence. And that presence is especially felt at Christmas when we celebrate the day God chose to come to earth in the form of a baby.

Concerning Jesus' ascension into heaven, Paul wrote, "For in him all the fullness of God was pleased to dwell, and through him to reconcile to himself all things, whether on earth or in heaven, making peace by the blood of his cross" (Colossians 1:19–20).

Just as Jesus possessed the power to bring peace to stormy seas (Matthew 8:26), He also brings peace between humans and peace between God and humans. As the Prince of Peace, He is the giver of peace. Although we are deserving of God's wrath, in His mercy, Jesus satisfied God's demands and declared peace between us.

As we live out that peace, and as we view each other as redeemed creatures by the same grace we received, we become more accepting of others and their ways. We love them for who they are, and not necessarily who we want them to be. We overlook more of their weaknesses because we understand weakness. We tolerate their bad days, because we've had many of our own.

The Prince of Peace has come, and He is in the process of making all things new. Rejoice in His presence today. Without Him, peace with God or other humans would not be possible.

FAMILY PRAYER TIME

For Families with Young Children:
Father, thank You for sending Your Son, the Prince of Peace, so that we could have peace with You. We know that without Jesus' birth and death, we would have no chance to be at peace with You. But since the Prince of Peace has come, we rejoice in knowing that He made peace for us. Amen.

For Families with Older Children:
Father, when we look at the many ways in which the world, and sometimes even the church, attempts to gain peace with each other, and with You, we are grieved. We know that no peace exists apart from Jesus. But as the Christmas season comes to a close, our family is still rejoicing over the birth of the Prince of Peace. Amen.

For Unto Us a Child Is Born
Words by Susan H. Peterson

For unto us a child is born,
To us a son is giv'n;
The government shall rest on him,
Th' anointed One from heav'n.
His name is Wonderful Counselor,
The Mighty God is He,
The Everlasting Father,
The humble Prince of Peace.

The increase of his government
And peace shall never end;
He'll reign on David's ancient throne
As ruler of all men.
Upheld with justice and righteousness,
Forever his kingdom will last;
The zeal of the Lord God Most High
Will bring these things to pass.

Lord Jesus, come now and reign in me,
Be Lord of my life this hour.
Come be my Counselor and my God,
My source of wisdom and power.
Watch o'er me with your Father care,
My heart and my mind, fill with peace.
I worship you, my Lord and King,
My praise will never cease.

LIVING THE EXPERIENCE

Family Discussion Topics:

🌿 How does Jesus bring peace between people?

🌿 How does Jesus bring peace between God and people?

🌿 Do you know anyone with whom you need to make peace? How might this devotion help you?

Family Activities:

🌿 Listen to Handel's *Messiah* again (as we did on December 6, December 13, and December 20 when we studied the idea of Jesus being the Wonderful Counselor, the Mighty God, and the Everlasting Father), and allow family members to worship the Prince of Peace however they choose.

🌿 If you need to make peace with somebody, do it today.

DECEMBER 28

CHRISTMAS PRAYERS: SUPPLICATION

Do not be anxious about anything,
but in everything by prayer and supplication
with thanksgiving let your requests
be made known to God.
PHILIPPIANS 4:6

FAMILY PRAYER

Father, as we near the end of the Christmas season, we have many prayer requests in our hearts. First, we ask that You would give our family the spirit of Christmas all year long. We want to live each day knowing that Your Son has come to give us new life.

Give us a desire to study Your Word more deeply this coming year. As we've looked at the way You've fulfilled Christmas prophecies, we've been encouraged in our faith, and we want more of that, Lord.

Give us a spirit of service all year. As we've read stories about families who found ways to serve You at Christmas, we've been encouraged to serve You more.

Give us a spirit of Christmas worship that lasts all year long. As much as we love worshiping during the Christmas season, we want to experience You more every day.

Give us a spirit of evangelism, just as the shepherds, apostle Paul, and Jesus had in the verses we studied.

Help us to remember the names of the Messiah as found in Isaiah 9:6. For Christ really is the Wonderful Counselor, Mighty God, Everlasting Father, and Prince of Peace. Amen.

GOING DEEPER PRAYER

Father, we know the incarnation to be an event that is beyond our ability to grasp. At the same time, though, we know it to be an event that changed the course of history. May we never lose the wonder of Christmas.

Help us never to relegate the celebration of Jesus' birth to once a year as the world celebrates. Instead, may we celebrate His birth continually.

May we never think about what we're going to receive, but rather how we can meet the needs of others.

May we never grow tired of reading and telling the Christmas story. For we know that the gospel is the power of God for salvation for everyone who believes.

May we continue to drink deeply of Your Word as we seek to know Your character more and as we seek to know Your ways. For we know that without Your Word, we drift through life, devoid of purpose.

May the new Christmas traditions that we've started this year continue many years into the future. We pray that You would use our feeble efforts to advance Your kingdom for many generations to come. Amen.

MAKING IT PERSONAL

Just as the apostle Paul instructed us not to be anxious about anything but instead to let our requests be made known to God, consider lifting up these specific supplications to Him:

- A deeper, more structured plan for studying the Word in the coming year.

- A way that you can meet the need of one person you haven't been able to help before.

- A resolve to continue your family Christmas traditions far into the future.

- A chance to share the Christmas story with one

person with whom you've never shared your faith.

᙮ An enthusiasm to worship all year the way you do during Christmas.

᙮ A daily awareness of the incarnation and what it means to you.

CLOSING FAMILY PRAYER

Father, we've brought our requests to You, and we know that You have been faithful to hear them. Now we pray the words of Jesus when He asked that Your will be done.

As we've set aside time as a family this Christmas to study more about You and the miracle of the virgin birth, You've brought us closer together and made us more aware of ways that we can live the Christmas experience. Father, gone is the feeling that Christmas has passed us by again.

Keep our family focused on the simplicity and also the complexity of the incarnation as we begin to think about the coming year. We don't want this precious time that we've spent together to slip from our memories or our routines.

The moment we pack away the last of the decorations, may You awaken within us a desire and excitement for the time when we will once again unpack them and, much more importantly, when we begin the countdown again toward the day we celebrate Your miraculous birth.

Father, may this Christmas be the one that we look back upon many years from now and say, "That was the Christmas we starting living the holiday, and we haven't stopped since." Amen.

DECEMBER 29

EXPERIENCE CHRISTMAS ALL YEAR: THE CHRISTMAS ATTITUDE

According to [God's] great mercy, he has caused us to be born again to a living hope through the resurrection of Jesus Christ from the dead, to an inheritance that is imperishable, undefiled, and unfading, kept in heaven for you.
1 PETER 1:3-4

FAMILY DEVOTION

I know a woman named Lane who left the church but then came back after thinking about something she heard from a minister. Years earlier, the minister had challenged her and other students in her Christian school by asking them what they thought Christmas meant.

After getting the standard "It's about Jesus" or "It's all about the presents" answers, the minister gave his own answer. Christmas, he said, was about the joy of knowing that because of Jesus' birth, he would live forever with Christ. According to the minister, knowing that was like having the thrill of Christmas morning every day.

"The minister's message never left me—it resonated in the core of my being," Lane said. "And when I finally found my way back to God and the church years later, I reexamined the message.

"I concluded that Christmas is about joy, and true joy only comes when one lives a life that is focused on Christ, while yearning for the day when we are able to spend forever with the One who made us. This joy need not be felt only one day a year, but every day of our lives; therefore, like the minister said, every day can contain the thrill of Christmas."

GOING DEEPER

The apostle Peter wrote his first epistle to a group of exiled Christians in Pontus, Galatia, Cappadocia, Asia, and Bithynia. Many Bible commentators believe that these Christians were descendants of Israelite captives from Babylon. Another school of thought says that these believers might have been in exile because of the persecution that took place after the death of Stephen.

Whatever the case, Peter knew that they had experienced hardships, and so he encouraged them with thoughts of eternity. He referred to eternity as "an inheritance that is imperishable, undefiled, and unfading, kept in heaven for you" (1 Peter 1:4).

You and I probably don't face exile or persecution. We do face trials, though. We experience the heartache when a loved one dies. We become anxious when we lose our jobs or change schools. We endure financial hardships from time to time. We move and have to make new friends. Some of us are estranged from people we love through no fault of our own, and we feel completely alone.

Experience Christmas anew today. Just as the minister subtly challenged Lane and her class, and just as Peter gently challenged the saints who were scattered abroad to think about eternity, I lovingly challenge you to do the same today.

That doesn't mean your pain won't be real. And it doesn't mean that you won't still need to seek guidance from God about how to handle your specific situation. Remember that life here on earth is but a vapor. We are here for a little while, and then we are gone (James 4:14). Eternity is forever.

Christmas Day has come and gone, and, sadly, most people won't think about it again anytime soon. For the Christian, however, every day can be Christmas as we think about our lives in light of the manger. Christmas is the day that God humbled Himself to come to earth and save wayward people.

Living with eternity in mind will help you to remember that just as God had a plan to redeem you, He also has a plan to sustain you during your current trials. And at the end of your trials lies eternity.

FAMILY PRAYER TIME

For Families with Young Children:

Father, help us to treat today and every day like it is Christmas. Life is short. Eternity is forever. We ask You to help us remember this whenever we start to think more about our problems than we do about where we will spend eternity. Amen.

For Families with Older Children:

Father, no matter how difficult our trials may be, remind us that You are our provider and sustainer while we are here, and that when our lives here on earth are finished, we will spend eternity with You. Help us to have the Christmas spirit all year long by living with eternity in mind. Amen.

Joy to the World
Words by Isaac Watts

Joy to the world, the Lord is come!
Let earth receive her King;
Let every heart prepare Him room,
And Heaven and nature sing,
And Heaven and nature sing,
And Heaven, and Heaven, and nature sing.

Joy to the earth, the Savior reigns!
Let men their songs employ;
While fields and floods, rocks, hills and plains
Repeat the sounding joy,
Repeat the sounding joy,
Repeat, repeat, the sounding joy.

No more let sins and sorrows grow,
Nor thorns infest the ground;
He comes to make His blessings flow
Far as the curse is found,
Far as the curse is found,
Far as, far as, the curse is found.

He rules the world with truth and grace,
And makes the nations prove
The glories of His righteousness,
And wonders of His love,
And wonders of His love,
And wonders, wonders, of His love.

Family Discussion Topics:

❧ Did the minister's message to Lane and her classmates challenge you to think about Christmas differently? If so, how?

❧ What does it mean to live every day like it is Christmas?

❧ How can living with eternity in mind help you to keep your current problems in perspective?

Family Activities:

❧ Write the text from 1 Peter 1:3–4 on an index card and resolve to carry it with you to remind you to live each day with eternity in mind.

❧ Choose a favorite hymn that deals with eternity or the joy felt at Christmastime and memorize the words.

DECEMBER 30

EXPERIENCE CHRISTMAS ALL YEAR: CHRIST IN US

*For we who live are always being given over to
death for Jesus' sake, so that the life of Jesus also
may be manifested in our mortal flesh.*
2 CORINTHIANS 4:11

FAMILY DEVOTION

You know that Christmas is about God showing us His love by sending His Son to earth. But Christmas Day was just the beginning for God's Son. You see, Jesus was born to die.

After He died and rose from the grave, Jesus established His church, ascended into heaven, and sent the Holy Spirit to earth. Here's how the apostle Paul describes what the Holy Spirit does:

"We rejoice in our sufferings, knowing that suffering produces endurance, and endurance produces character, and character produces hope, and hope does not put us to shame, because God's love has been poured into our hearts through the Holy Spirit who has been given to us" (Romans 5:3–5).

The original Christmas Day leads up to today as the Holy Spirit works to change us from people who are self-centered into people of God. As the Holy Spirit works in us, according to today's verse, the life of Jesus becomes manifested, or seen by others, in us.

While the day we celebrate as Christmas is gone for this year, we can live every day as if it were Christmas. The earthly work that God started through Jesus continues every day until Jesus returns.

GOING DEEPER

A couple of days after my dad died in 2000, I read a quote that helped me: "Life is for the living." Suddenly I felt permission to grieve and then pick up the pieces to begin living again—without one of my parents.

After losing a loved one, people tend to feel like they aren't supposed to "live" again. They feel indebted to the person they lost because that person meant so much to them. They feel that they can't return to a "normal" life for an extended period of time. Sometimes after people lose loved ones, they even allow the hopes or expectations that the loved one had for their life to dictate how they live.

I didn't allow that to happen. By God's grace, I knew that I was supposed to be living my life based on the expectations of another who preceded me in death—Jesus. And in that sense, I joined with millions of others who have called upon the name of Jesus, in "being given over to death for Jesus' sake, so that the life of Jesus also may be manifested in our mortal flesh."

The little baby who was born in Bethlehem and placed in a manger grew up to pay the ultimate price for my sins and yours. And in the process, He set in motion the work of the Holy Spirit that drew us to Himself to regenerate our souls and ultimately to transform us from people who were dead in sin to people who turn from sin daily by the power of the Spirit.

As such, every day is like Christmas. We prayerfully start each day anew with certain plans and agendas, and then Jesus begins His transforming work and redirects our steps. As we submit to the Spirit's direction, our old nature is being put to death. And unlike the unhealthy situation where we allow the expectations of a deceased loved one to dictate our actions, we are controlled by Christ—who overcame the grave.

Christianity as we know it didn't end on Christmas Day. It started there and it continues every day of every year. While Christmas Day is a joyous occasion for believers, our everyday lives are to manifest the risen Christ.

FAMILY PRAYER TIME

For Families with Young Children:

Father, we've spent a lot of time this last month celebrating the birth of Your Son. As we begin to think about the New Year, we know that Christmas is more than just a one-time event. As the Holy Spirit works in us each day, we experience the miracle of Christmas. Thank You for allowing us to experience Christmas all year long. Amen.

For Families with Older Children:

Father, we desire to become more like Jesus every day and we're grateful that Your Spirit is at work within us. Help us to see Christmas Day as a remembrance of the day you began the redemption process that continues as You transform every area of our lives. Amen.

Celebrate Immanuel's Name
Words by Charles Wesley

Celebrate Immanuel's Name, the Prince of life and peace.
God with us, our lips proclaim, our faithful hearts confess.
God is in our flesh revealed; Heav'n and earth in Jesus join.
Mortal with Immortal filled, and human with Divine.

Fullness of the Deity in Jesus' body dwells,
Dwells in all His saints and me when God His Son reveals.
Father, manifest Thy Son; breathe the true incarnate Word.
In our inmost souls make known the presence of the Lord.

Let the Spirit of our Head through every member flow;
By our Lord inhabited, we then Immanuel know.
Then He doth His Name express; God in us we truly prove,
Find with all the life of grace and all the power of love.

Family Discussion Topics:

❧ In what way was Jesus born to die?

❧ How is the first Christmas connected to the Holy Spirit's work in believers today?

❧ According to 2 Corinthians 4:11, what must happen in a Christian's life before Christ will be manifested in him or her?

Family Activities:

❧ Read Romans 5:3–5 and spend some time thinking about ways you have reacted during times of suffering. How are we supposed to react, according to these verses?

❧ Think about an area where your character is weak. Silently pray for the Spirit to transform these weaknesses into strengths and to give you the endurance you need.

DECEMBER 31

EXPERIENCE CHRISTMAS ALL YEAR: FORGETTING WHAT IS PAST

But one thing I do: forgetting what lies behind and straining forward to what lies ahead, I press on toward the goal for the prize of the upward call of God in Christ Jesus.
PHILIPPIANS 3:13-14

FAMILY DEVOTION

After Christmas is over, we naturally begin to think about the New Year. What surprises will God bring into our lives? How will next year be different from this year? And here's the biggie—how do we get past the mistakes we made this year so we can be ready for God to use us in the coming year?

The first two questions are up to God and the last question is up to us. We don't need to look far to find the answer—it's all about Christmas. Jesus was born and then died to pay the penalty for our sin (so we wouldn't have to). That's what the apostle Paul is referring to in today's verse. As a Christian who confessed his sin to God, Paul left his old sins in the past so he could focus on the call that God had on his future.

You know that excited feeling you get on Christmas Eve? I think Paul felt that way when he wrote these verses. And he received the greatest gift of all—salvation. Paul wanted to live each new day like it was Christmas with God's mercy in mind.

GOING DEEPER

When the apostle Paul warned the Philippian church about "evildoers" (Philippians 3:2), he told them to rejoice in Christ "and have no confidence in the flesh." As a former circumcised Pharisee from the tribe of Benjamin, Paul once placed a great deal of confidence in his fleshly works. Now he pointed to his faith in the work of Christ as the means for his salvation (Philippians 3:9).

He was so in love with what Jesus had done for him

that he was willing to suffer "the loss of all things and count them as rubbish" (Philippians 3:8). Paul even wanted to know the power of the resurrection by sharing in Christ's sufferings, and becoming more like Him in his death (Philippians 3:10).

But Paul also wanted to make sure that the Philippian church didn't get the wrong idea about what he was saying. He went on to say that even though he hadn't obtained perfection, he was pressing on, in spite of his past sins, toward the One who is perfect.

Every year at this time most of us reflect about the past year and the new one to come. We probably have regrets about our past sins, and we think about our hopes for the future. At times we wonder if we've made too many mistakes, and committed too many sins, to dare dream about the future.

Paul considered himself to be the chief of sinners (1 Timothy 1:15). He admitted once to being "a blasphemer, persecutor, and insolent opponent" of God (1 Timothy 1:13). As Luke pointed out in Acts 8:1, Paul (then called Saul) approved of Stephen's stoning.

If Paul can find such mercy and forgiveness for his past sins, then surely you and I can, too. And if his sins of blasphemy and persecution to the point of authorizing murder didn't stop him from pressing on "toward the goal for the prize of the upward call of God in Christ Jesus," our sins shouldn't stop us either.

The mercy that Paul received came to earth as a baby who was the sinless, spotless Lamb, who took away the sins of the world. And from the moment of Paul's conversion in Acts 9, he set out to live each day like it was Christmas by walking in God's mercy. He didn't always succeed (see Romans 7:14–24), but he was quick to admit his sins and run back to the Source of all mercy. Remember Paul's example as you begin the new year.

FAMILY PRAYER TIME

For Families with Young Children:
Father, we want to start the new year right. If we have any sins we haven't confessed, we ask that You would bring them to our minds. Please help us see that each day, and each year, is a new chance to live for You. Amen.

For Families with Older Children:
Father, we know that we've made mistakes this past year, and we know that we've grieved Your Holy Spirit with sin that so easily entangled us. Help us to heed Paul's call to forget what lies behind us so we can press on toward the prize You've set before us. Help us to live each day of the coming year with the mercy of Christ in mind so that each day can feel like Christmas. Amen.

Another Year Is Dawning
Words by Frances R. Havergal

Another year is dawning, dear Father, let it be
In working or in waiting, another year with Thee.
Another year of progress, another year of praise,
Another year of proving Thy presence all the days.

Another year of mercies, of faithfulness and grace,
Another year of gladness in the shining of Thy face;
Another year of leaning upon Thy loving breast;
Another year of trusting, of quiet, happy rest.

Another year of service, of witness for Thy love,
Another year of training for holier work above.
Another year is dawning, dear Father, let it be
On earth, or else in Heaven, another year for Thee.

Family Discussion Topics:

- ❧ Do you ever feel like the sins you have committed are too bad for God to forgive? Has this devotion changed your mind?

- ❧ What are your family's hopes and dreams for the coming year? Are you willing to commit them to prayer, asking God for guidance and direction?

- ❧ What did Paul mean by the phrase "press on toward the goal"?

Family Activities:

- ❧ Take five to ten minutes to write down your goals for living differently this next year. Then share what you've written with your family.

- ❧ After making a copy of what you've written, pool your lists of goals and seal them in an envelope. Open the envelope at this same time next year to see how well you've pressed on.